a

book

of

uncommon

prayer

MW00426699

an anthology of everyday invocations edited by matthew vollmer

Outpost19 | San Francisco
outpost19.com

Copyright 2015 by Matthew Vollmer.
Published 2015 by Outpost19.
All rights reserved.

Vollmer, Matthew (ed.)
        A Book of Uncommon Prayer / Matthew Vollmer,
editor
        ISBN 9781937402761 (pbk)
        ISBN 9781937402778 (ebk)

Library of Congress Control Number: 2015902711

Proceeds from this book benefit 826 Valencia. 826 Valencia
is a nonprofit organization dedicated to supporting
students ages six to eighteen with their creative and
expository writing skills and to helping teachers inspire
their students to write. Their services are structured around
the understanding that great leaps in learning can happen
with one-on-one attention and that strong writing skills are
fundamental to future success.

OUTPOST19

PROVOCATIVE READING
SAN FRANCISCO
NEW YORK
OUTPOST19.COM

A
BOOK
OF
UNCOMMON
PRAYER

Merry Christmas 2015!

Matthew Vollmer

12/10/15

Table of Contents

Preface

As soon as I could talk my mother taught me how to pray. I prayed on my knees by my bed at night and if my mind went blank, she whispered words to help me along. I prayed in church, both silently and—when reciting the Lord's Prayer—aloud. I prayed at school, folding my hands over my lunch box and thanking God for my food. I recited prayers and memory verses—Psalm 23, Isaiah 40:31, John 3:16—with my classmates. I asked God to watch over my family. I thanked him for my sister and our dogs and for my very own personal guardian angel. I asked Him to make my grandfather—who'd suffered a stroke—better. I asked him to help me remember facts and figures so that I might do well on my tests, to help me find my lost wallet or misplaced orthodonture. Nothing was too large or too small to warrant a prayer. God's eyes were on the sparrow. He was watching over me as well.

I don't know when my prayers started to feel obligatory. I can't pinpoint a moment where I, as someone who was addressing the Divine Other, became self-conscious, or when I recognized something phony in my petitions. It certainly didn't happen overnight. But it happened.

It wasn't that I stopped believing in God. It was that I started re-imagining Who or What God might be. Asking the Source of All Life to send his angels to watch over me as I drove—a prayer my father and mother said before embarking upon long trips—or to help me find my keys or my phone or to alter the events of the day so that, in the end, things would turn out in my favor, seemed presumptuous and self-centered. Not that I wasn't—and not that I'm not—self-centered. I just wasn't convinced that God—as the mysterious and omniscient sustainer of the universe—could be called upon to function as a sort of everyday Santa Claus in the sky, dispensing blessings only upon those who knew how to submit the proper petitions.

II.

The first time I became aware of the power of the *Book of Common Prayer* was on a Sunday morning in Monroe, North Carolina, in the church where my wife and I had been married. I was standing next to my stepmother-in-law, a woman whose southern accent and idiosyncratic grammar ("Don't he look like his daddy?" and "Ya'll ain't leaving yet are you?") I might've described as representative of many people I knew who'd grown up in my home state. But when she repeated the prayers in the *Book of Common Prayer*—without even cracking open the book, as she appeared to have memorized each and every one that the parishioners recited that day—she pronounced words with a solemn and resonant precision. The languid flow of her "everyday voice"—in which words seemed to ooze from one into another—was now characterized by sharply defined pronunciation. It almost seemed as if the words of the prayer book were inhabiting—and thus, momentarily, possessing—her body. Though I have no doubt that she believed the prayers to be manifestations of her particular beliefs, it seems unlikely that, without the aid of the *Book of Common Prayer*, she would've been able to articulate herself with such exactness and economy. One might say that her speech moved from sphere of the domestic—a place ruled, it seemed, by the recycling of everyday slang and idiomatic banter—into the realm of the mystical, where language was charged but sober, terrestrial but divine.

III.

I'd grown up in the Seventh-day Adventist church—a denomination that honored the tradition of extemporaneous prayer. When kneeling during a service, one wasn't ever quite sure where a pastor's linguistic meanderings might lead, and thus, when such an entreaty—powered by the speaker's desire to construct a substantial address—might end. Not so in the Anglican Church. Most prayers appear on a specific page of the *Book of Common Prayer*; as such, they enter the eyes and the ears, and one can read and follow along. The book's preface, written in 1789, reveals that its aims are to express "what the truths of the Gospel are; and earnestly beseeching Almighty God to accompany with his blessing every endeavor for promulgating them to mankind in the clearest, plainest, most affecting and majestic manner." A lofty goal, perhaps, but one that, I discovered, in reading these petitions, seemed achievable. The prayers were lyrical but measured. Evocative, yet clear. Earnest, but never sentimental. Heartfelt, but reasonable. These prayers, they often sounded to my ears like poetry. Like literature. And the more I thought about it, the more that made sense. Prayers— regardless of what they might attempt to express—are made up of words. Of language. So why shouldn't those of us who pray take care to ensure that ours resemble pretty little houses for our hopes and dreams to live?

IV.

There's a section in the *Book of Common Prayer* called "Prayers and Thanksgivings." In it, one finds prayers with titles like, "For all Sorts of Conditions of Man," "For Our Enemies," "For Sound Government," "For Social Justice," "For Agriculture," "For Those Who Live Alone." These prayers, as expressions of fundamental human concerns, have—I'd argue—the power to transform awareness and elevate consciousness, regardless of whether a reader considers him or herself a believer. If nothing else, the prayers promote a spirit of humility by directing a reader's thoughts toward a world made of—and lived in—by others. Ornate but never ostentatious, they request that we be lead—along with our enemies—from "prejudice to truth," or that lawmakers might fulfill their obligations "in the community of nations," or "that barriers which divide us may crumble, suspicions disappear, and hatreds cease." Reciting them, one can indulge the notion that it might be possible to speak reality into being.

V.

I started this project with the thought that it would become an homage to the *Book of Common Prayer*. I also assumed that I would write every prayer in it. But when I mentioned the idea to my friend Courtney Maum, a writer whose work I admire a great deal, and who I provided with a list of possible titles, she asked—excitedly—if I might open it to other contributors, because she would love the chance to write one about the guy who "drives the little truck behind the wide load trailer." Hm, I thought. Interesting. Maybe I shouldn't try to write them all myself. Perhaps I should enlist other writers whose work I admired to help. After all, the original Book of Common Prayer had been composed by a group of writers. Why not construct this one in a similar spirit?

I invited potential contributors without regard to—and, in most cases, no knowledge whatsoever of—their religious inclinations; I simply wanted to see what happened when writers confronted the assignment of writing a prayer. I encouraged them to write about topics that were "uncommon"—that is, things and people and places that might not usually be prayed for. I wanted to see what happened when poets and writers of literary prose entered this particular form, how they'd push against the conventions to make something new, and—hopefully—expand the notion of prayer as a genre. The result, I'm pleased to report, is a book of prayers that is as diverse as its contributors. There are angry prayers, earnest prayers, sarcastic prayers, funny prayers, prayers somber and prayers joyful. There are prayers that address everyday concerns—such as children in rear-facing safety seats, gluten, flight attendants, or the deactivation of Facebook accounts—and prayers that explore more extraordinary subjects—like alien abductees, actors in pornographic films, and the unlikely heroes of apocalypse movies. While many of the prayers reveal themselves to be the work of atheists, agnostics, or steadfast believers, many of them unfold in ways that refuse to disclose the writers' religious affiliations. I like not knowing. I enjoy inhabiting the faith of the devout just as much as I like inhabiting the doubt of an unbeliever. After all, prayer—as a genre, as a rhetorical mode—encompasses so much of what we writers struggle with everyday: the attempt at expression, the articulation of desires, the hope of resolution. The prayers in this book are spaces of repose, of curiosity, wonder, and regret. They are meant to be seen, but also to be read aloud, not only because they were meant to live in the body, but also to be heard by others, in the hope that those hearers may—if only for a moment—experience the transformations that accompany the honest and clear expressions of what it means to be alive.

— Matthew Vollmer, editor

A Bidding Prayer for Those Who Pray

To be used before reading.

(mostly) GOOD People, I bid your prayers for the blessed
company of all faithful people who pray; that it may please the
Reader to confirm and strengthen it in purity of heart, in holiness of life, and perfectness of play, and to restore to it the
witness of visible unity among those who yearn for Saturday
mail and those who ache to sink the winning free throw in a
championship game one only ever imagines to be playing while
shooting at the hoop with a chain link net behind the church;
and more especially for that branch of those who long for wings
not just for show or to imply one can fly, but to prove; whereof
we are all members with late fees that once walked the near
extinct aisles of video stores trying to remember the movie they
reminded themselves they needed to see again or for the first
time, but forgot; that in all things may work according to some
goodness behind a curtain, serve said entity faithfully, and worship what it means to worship acceptably without fail.

What Is Good: A Meditation

The way the winter sky is both sunny and ominous, this is good. All things that are ambiguous but reliable are good. Foods that take decades to be appealing, like turnips and beets, are good. Records that you hate at first are good. Paintings that you don't understand for years, but which then reveal their intensities, very good. The weird ebbing and surging of long friendship is good. Things that disappear and then reappear are good, socks being one example. Things seen backwards through binoculars are good. Waiting is good. Waiting even longer is better. Extremely long dull waiting periods when you imagine you will never do anything but wait, these are hellish, but sometimes good. Sleeping with someone and forgetting about the explosive part of it, this is often good and refreshing. Remembering that there was a thing you wanted to do, and then forgetting it, this is often very good. Youth is good when you are young, but middle age is much much better, much more good, and in middle age youth seems vain and self-satisfied, except in certain exceptional cases. Blurry photographs are better than photographs that are distinct. Stories in which the narrative is all but absent are extremely good. Indistinct narrators are good. People who come back into your life after long intervals, with apologies, are absolutely good. Pieces of music that do the same things over and over, until in the repetition you begin to see that the repeated thing has infinitely more variety than you hitherto believed, these pieces of music are so good that we need to laud and magnify them. The repetition of the word "good" until it is drained of significant meaning is good. "Good," since it is overused by children early in the learning curve of language acquisition, needs to be made *good* all over again. Virtue is good and virtue when stippled with failure is even better. The acknowledgment of earthly failure is always good. Ideals are essential, but lapsed ideals are nearly as good. Good is perhaps derived from Sanskrit *gadh*, to hold fast, which implies that uniting is good. Bearing things together when they are apart is good, finding the order in the disparate is good; people with extremely large eyes are good, laughing in the dark is good, and whispering is good and all silences are good, as are the times after silence. Plato is good, Aristotle is less good, Neitzsche is good in some ways. Fear of death is often very, very good. But only up to a point. Making up things as you go along is a good way of working and then rearranging the order of these things very quickly without looking is also good. Your insides are good, your organs and viscera, your inmost longing, and you should let them be outside, this would be good, at least in some metaphorical way.

The Lord's Prayer

Our Father freely roaming in heaven, that place which seemed to be around the corner, upstairsward, when we were children, a place endlessly unraveling like a fugitive's sleeve caught on barbed wire...

We sing out your name, these days, to what still moves us: a sunlight-exposed room like the answer to a question that doesn't dare to be formed, sand on the palms of children where sand belongs, the quiet backs of stones illuminating the dark, the crickets that carry that dark far out to the crannies of the night, the sunset hitting only half of the mountain like a life that could have been lived more than one way.

May your kingdom be seen by all, LORD, for what it is, right here on earth – the quiet night migrations above just as traffic through city's arteries begins to slither; a mother's breast that, like a drop of sun, sets behind the cloud of her purple shirt when the child falls asleep; the moment when, lying down starlike on the grass looking at stars, we fall in love with ourselves for the first time; this dog that you have given us (who manages to come up at this time, in this prayer, like a referee of truth) guarding from behind a window – guarding what, if not that very kingdom he, too, notices outside – the quiet night migrations above...

We pray your will be done since our own is known to take us only as far as the next bed.

Give us this day our daily collection of losses. Help us receive the fact that lovers who leave will remain friends only until they can no longer remain. Life's an arrangement except the flowers are small little deaths. When the fog falls over the lake we see the fog. We see the lake. We miss the scenery – solitude, time for You, LORD, to rest Your feet where we and all those lovers once laid our heads.

And forgive us
And forgive us
And forgive us
And those who
And those who beat us and told us we're nothing.

But frankly, LORD, there are no mistakes. Only choices in a universe where if we open one door, we've opened them all the way to the end.

Lead us not into the light, just yet, for in the dark we grope our way toward You, which is to say we continue to arrive at ourselves. Deliver us from fear, LORD, straight through to the other side... love, is it?

For yours is everything, Father: our houses, our breaths, dead skin, clipped fingernails, this dog's hairs twined into our car seats and rugs. Even the last "e" (on the window of which you sometimes perch resting your thin, beautiful chin on your palms) at the end of this sentence. Nothing belongs to us. We open our hands and give it all back to you the way the sky opens this late August night - an old Maria shaking out her tablecloth offering stars for breadcrumbs. Forever and always we give you back what's yours, Father. Even that which you haven't given us. Even that which you can't help but take. *Amen.*

A Sophist's Prayer

With not great humility I offer this prayer for forgiveness
to the biosphere, planet, the future, and/or the universe.
Not that the universe could possibly care. No, perhaps not
so much a prayer but a request, a respectful request, such
as one might make to a complex and sensitive bureaucracy
with its codes, regulations, forms, deadlines, sanctions,
penalties, and its website that no single human has ever
succeeded in fully exploring, a bureaucracy that has now
and then been compared to a black hole. It has been said
that those who retire from it after thirty years of servitude
to its bits and pixels have commonly lost the power of
speech.

So, a request, or a series of requests, uttered with the sense
that perhaps none of them will fit the exacting protocols
of the receiving agency, or agencies. And with the understanding that like all requests this one may only call attention to myself and actually worsen the situations I am
attempting to be forgiven for—no, excused from. I have
often said that it's not my fault that I was born into a
world of such unsatisfactory design and construction. In
this sense we are all illegal immigrants. Or some of us at
least.

My request to be excused is the effect of finally understanding the nature of the human condition, or more
particularly, *my personal human condition*, as a sentient, intelligent, educated being of impeccable good taste within
a world that has little or no use for my particular subspe-
cies or genera. A world rapacious, predatory, voracious,

tasteless, and insensitive. A world in short one can hardly pray to, let alone request from—without sullying oneself; a world to which one can only casually cast backhanded suggestions, recommendations, *hints*.

So, that said, I would like to propose the following hints of the things that perhaps, and only perhaps, I am worthy of being forgiven, if it is somehow, eventually, in the grand ledger of things, that in these areas I have sinned in some conventional old-fashioned sense or have overstepped some boundary once thought sacred or have generally been found wanting.

A small caveat here: with few or no exceptions I have stayed within the consumption parameters of a typical middle class American, so that I cannot be condemned, including self-condemnation here, not my strong-point, for practices shared by tens of millions of fellow—so to speak—citizens. This is you might say a Class-Action argument: touch one and you touch all.

So that these requests, or hints of requests, are made in a somewhat provisional manner, in the event that in the Final Reckoning all these tens of millions are waved away with a flick of a pontifical wrist—a metaphor here, nothing else—and thereby told to go stand in the other line over there, the one that moves rapidly right along towards a final destination, no security checks, no passports or tickets needed, no prying questions by customs officials. And where, once in that line, the good line, one breathes a sign of relief and realizes that all those hypothetical prayers to be forgiven—no, excused—all those requests, hints tickling

one's tongue and ready to be spilled out, that all that fret-
ting was entirely unnecessary, and indeed a waste of time
and energy.

As one's last secret weapon, there are the folded banknotes
in the breast pocket of the sports coat, which could be so
easily slipped into the palm of the complicit official, who
would know the correct angle at which to position his
body to foil the prying eyes of a half-dozen video cameras.

In bribing my way to forgiveness of course I do add a
little twist, the need to be forgiven for the bribe. But of
course this never ends, but I wasn't the one who invented
a world—a future—a planet—a biosphere—a universe in
which *it never ends*.

A Creed

We believe in one God or another, the God of Heaven and Hell, provider of divine scripture, an unequivocal God of expectation and punishment, His word final, infallible. Or we believe in no such thing, in many things.

We believe in Stuff. Through our stuff we seek salvation. Sedans ensnared in backyard weeds, small businesses – brokerage firm, used car lot, bike shop – and beer steins. Or G.I. Joes. We believe G.I. Joe rose from his packaging in a smaller form, that we might talk.

> Joe isn't what he used to be.
> Yeah, now he has muscles.

We believe in Food: fourth pork chop and sneaked bites before bed, no matter gout, never mind cholesterol. Or microwaved leftovers during after-school cartoons and whole bags of Cool Ranch in one afternoon.

And Drink: Miller Genuine Draft or Dr. Pepper by the twelve pack.

We believe in Music, in boozing with The Platters or smoking to *In Utero*. In nostalgic late-night clarinet twice each year or half-learned guitar behind a closed bedroom door.

We believe in Burdens. For our sake our worlds weigh upon us, that we might suffer, might lash out, might forever distrust, dislike ourselves and each other. To stresses and disappointments we turn, the better to hurt as we most deeply believe we deserve to hurt.

We believe in Work. We assemble Chinese tractors in a garage full of fenders and frames hauled from Houston, spend a summer eating lunch specials at a small diner, talking shop over Possum Pie.

But you are nothing without too much work to do, and I have school and, soon, a son of my own.

We believe in Signs, in hiking Arkansas' Mount Nebo and asking God to reveal Himself. Opening our eyes, we accept as affirmation the unlikely genius of a timely Walking Stick.

Or we take such faith as a sign in itself.

We believe in Independence, squeezing lime into coozied beer on the Fourth, playing catch with our sons in the pool before debating, again, the fate of our nation, our jokes lighting fuses that burn to the bomb, blow us apart, make birthday phone calls briefer.

We believe in the Father we won't live to be, a man who guides and teaches, calmly, with devotion. At your grandson's blessing, you regret not leading me to God and I thank God you didn't as men bend over my child and strangely pray.

Prayer of the Agnostic

LORD, thank you
for my doubt you exist and my certainty
I'm being watched by eyes of clouds and eyes
of doorknobs when I dream or masturbate,
when I insist upon harmony or recoil
from accord with a hammer against the knees
of my neighbor, with nails in my throat
as I run up the mountain to lean my breath
against the possibility that you dwell
within the disguise of air. Wondering
if you're there has made it more interesting
to be stoned, more challenging
to find "God damn it" transgressive,
and the time I rode my bike in church,
I thought of you every lap—would you
spank me if you were real or climb on
and rip a bigassed "whee," like any deity
I'd want to have a catch with would.
Thank you for letting me get away with that
when I was eleven and curious about
where all sorts of things fit in, such as myself
and particularly that part of myself
that sometimes resembles a rudder
and most often looks sleepy and useless,
thank you for yo-yos while I'm at it,
and fog, and my wife, my wife,
who is not fog and believes in you
without question, whereas I wonder
if I could believe in question without you.
If you're there, you're busy, if you're not,
where is the there you're not, and is that
the non-place I'm headed, a pondering
only you can answer and you're one mute

mother-fucker, I say that with affection,
being something of an amateur hermit
myself. And here's the deal: someone
or something needs to be thanked
for the cornucopia, it might as well be you,
you who are everything or just a syllable,
who are life or an utterance we need
for the will to slink our way out
the door. Thanks for stars and making us
from what was left of stars when they retired
from light, thanks for the garage band
of crickets and the big band of waves
proffering their endless hallelujahs,
I'm a fan of your work, honestly everything
you've done or not done, from tapioca
to suicide, gravity to gravitas. Even the sharks
in the womb who eat other sharks
in the womb – thanks for how terribly
wonderfully creepy that is, for making that
part of the story we're told
by sunrise, told by tides
of nucleotides and the atom-smashing
of kids playing with their buckets
in sand, this has been, as they say, a hoot,
a wonder, a pain in the ass, thanks for the chance
to be the form of life, the loudspeaker
that puts the vastness into words,
into mumbles and songs and prayers
and swirls them possibly back to you
possibly listening, probably not.

For the Mysterious Source of Life

Oh Mysterious Source of Life,

I am happy that I do not know You personally.

I am thankful for life, though I believe, because of the way my brain works, that You did not consciously create life in the ways that many people have visualized life being created. Thus, complications arise with the word *Source*. Thank you for the word "that."

Help me to see life around me, and to distinguish life from not-life (as in money and stocks) though I realize that in the molecular universe we are finding distinctions between life and not-life more and more fuzzy. And I recognize how the need for food, shelter, and clothing among the poor—in view of the plentitude of those items among others who are no more worthy, and in some cases less worthy, than the poor—may drive the poor crazy, as it drove Jesus and other teachers, also poor, crazy. Thank you for the word *fuzzy*.

Or rather:

Thank you, Oh Mysterious Source of Life, for stepping back and allowing our species to invent—for our pleasure and comfort—words, phrases, clauses, sentences, musical instruments, entire paragraphs, good and bad books, war, and blogs.

Now. Looking back, may I forevermore say *I am thankful for* and *I am responsible or partly responsible for* rather than *Thank You for* as the formers may lead toward self-reliance and away from obstinacy. I am now thankful for the phrase "I am thankful for." Hadn't really thought about all that. I am thankful for the word *really*, most of the time. Really.

I observe, OMSOL, that sometimes we can't think up something without writing it down. I am thankful that I can observe.

I believe that this life is it, OMSOL&D, and given Your possible make up—as the Mysterious Source of Life & Death, not the Mysterious Source of Afterlife—I see that what we *call*

13

heaven doesn't exist as often explained in books and sermons. I am thankful for the phrase *that what*.

I do get that given your mystery, You could also be the Source of Afterlife, but I realize that you, as *source*, may not *know* (in the way I *know*) what you have done or not done—or do. I do appreciate You, as I have had a good life, so far. If you, too, *can* know in some sense, then you probably sense that many animals we kill and eat—or people we kill—could not generally appreciate life as in the leisurely same way as many others do: say, pets, or grown children of billionaires, or men and women who write commercials for children.

So what has come about seems to be a mixed bag.

And I think I know the reason that You, as *God*, have not, for me—as You did for The Hebrew Bible women and mostly men and other ancient-and-contemporary-religions-and-sects-of-the-world women and mostly men—made Yourself clearly known in all Your splendor. The reason is that it's not in your nature. And isn't it, OMSOL&D, perhaps true that those sometimes beautiful, psychological, and sociological, and plain smart stories were more or less made up? I am thankful for the word *nature*.

Glad for splendor, and thankful for that crafty concept *extrapolate*, I remain

Yours Truly.

An Agnostic or Maybe Atheist Hindu's Plea for Sanity, Or If That's Not Possible, Some Snacks

O whomsoever is up there,

You, and you, and you also, since you're simultaneously aspects of one—

—grant us patience with the bearded white hippie who, at the gym in suburbia, says *namaste* to us instead of hello, and thinks that for this he should receive karmic points, and perhaps even more hilariously, that we in our mystical brownness might be capable of distributing such, even though we know no one other than he who greets another person in this fashion;

> Or alternatively, make us capable of distributing such points, none of which shall go to him, but shall only go to people who have had *namaste* said to them unsolicitedly on the basis of race;

> > And should that be the case, may all such points be redeemable for fresh mangosteens, which we have had overseas but which are in any case only available on the black market in the United States, and who knows why, because they are delicious and might go far towards distracting from the irritations of unsolicited *namastes*;

> > > Or, since it must be said, the irritations of people assuming we do yoga, although we prefer soccer, which for some reason seems to surprise them;

And, o whomsoever is up there, give us the strength to bear

15

with the low-grade curry powder at the grocery store, which is so weak as to make us weep from lack of chili rather than its presence, being made for the concept of the bearded white hippie rather than for the actual we, and being shelved in the aisle of ethnicity, as it is so vaguely rendered;

> Or alternatively, and frankly this might be easier, make it actually spicy;

> Or alternatively again, or maybe even in addition, permit us to be correctly spice-profiled at all restaurants for the remainder of all our lives, should we be so fortunately reincarnated;

And, O god and God and God of gods, bestow upon us the wisdom to know that just because someone asks whether Hinduism is monotheistic or polytheistic does not mean that we have to answer the question, since in our opinion this is a ridiculous binary and also who died and made us the spokesperson for anything, least of all to a random dude at a random gym in a town where we don't live and are just on a visitor's pass anyway;

> Or alternatively, if we are to be constantly asked to be a native informant, may the questions and micro-aggressions at least be more intelligent, and may the person who died and made us spokesperson be reincarnated as a...

> But, o whomsoever is up there, make us not so ungracious and unkind, lest we also be reincarnated as something unpleasant that never gets to eat good food;

And O whomsoever is up there, maybe even Ganesha himself, give non-Hindus something other than Ganesha to use as a metaphor for multi-tasking, because although we have a special affection for his elephantine face, this usage wearies us so;

Or alternatively, may his image also be a universal symbol of the presence of very good food, since he is known to appreciate such;

And may we in our weariness stumble upon a place that makes tea properly and rejuvenates us with the strength of both caffeine and belief in you—

And O, when someone expresses great shock that our Asian parents did not insist that we all be doctors, let us be silent—

And let us go instead to the temple, whereupon we shall eat of the snacks that our "beautiful culture" has, in fact, so graciously provided, and let all the people there talk of social justice, and especially talk of caste and how its wrongs might be recognized and subsequently addressed;

Because you in your wisdom make generous allowance for bountiful meals in which we might take comfort, even if we occasionally and inconveniently do not believe in you because of seeing mostly injustice, which we understand some others term the problem of evil, and for which you no doubt have a solution;

And we guess, o whomsoever, that the arc of justice must be really long, and how many reincarnations are we going to need for this? Because when you come right down to it, that un-sought *namaste* is kind of the least of it;

And may the canteen of the temple deserve its four-star res-taurant review, being one of few religious institutions to be so reviewed; and may the yogurt rice and the sour rice and the crisp dosa be plentiful and cheap, and the chutneys and sauces and kulfis and puddings varied, and accompanied by fake im-ported mango juice and real coconut water, the kind you get from hacking into a young coconut with a machete, but very safely of course, under your benevolent protection;

And may you also enjoy what we have offered you, and next time we hope to be better and to do better,

And may the family at the next table include a little girl smaller than her dosa, who is not yet as jaded as us, though she be as hungry for what tastes good.

A Petition for Protection

Oh LORD protect us,

  when in rain, when in snow, when in the vicinity of thunder and thus lightning strikes, when in distress, when in a dress (from change-dropping up-skirt-lookers let us be devoid), when trying to impress, when stressed, when eating desserts, when fishing for compliments, when wanting to look good but not to be ogled, when climbing ladders to squat upon our roofs because the gutters are full again, when driving any length of time or distance, when goofing off, when fully functional, when drunk, when high, when snorting just one more line, when lighting up, when powering down, when showering in tubs without non-slip bath appliqués, when eating meat with fine bones or spinach that arrived in a plastic bag, when sleeping, when walking through the dark house toward a toilet, when cycling with or without a helmet, when singing lullabies, when soliciting our spouses for sex, when leaving ladders out in the rain, when forgetting to let the dog out at night, when waking to find that the dog needed to be let out, when yelling at the dog, when yelling at child who attempts to console dog, when looking at how money was spent last month, when not understanding where it all went, when considering selling one's house and moving into an apartment, when mixing one last cocktail, when mixing another, when swearing that this is the last month for cable television, when flipping off the kid who rolls down his window to ask if we saw the stop sign or not, when eating a late night snack, oh LORD we ask that you protect us of course from all that is evil, but most of all we ask that you protect us from ourselves.

The Prayers of the Person

For the house on Astor Lane where we grew up, and for the delay of that house's decline into ruin; for the strengthening of that house's roof, which looks very bad now when we go home to visit; for the removal of the several children's toys that have made their way onto the porch, though no child dwells inside; for the healing of the hot water heater whose pilot light goes out each week; or at least for the stay of its death, until our parents can afford to buy a new one—next month, says our mother, or maybe two months from now; for the dead piano, which has not been played in a decade, and which our father plans to sell; that it may fetch a good price; that he may remember to get it tuned first; let us pray.

For Mrs. Meredith, our old piano teacher, whose husband Ron Meredith died last month, according to our mother on the phone; for Mrs. Meredith, whom we loved, and whom we now imagine alone in the old house in which she taught us, playing the saddest songs she knows; for the piano of Mrs. Meredith; for its endurance and well-being, and for the continuing loyalty of her students to her; and for the hands of Mrs. Meredith, which were already distended with arthritis when we took lessons from her fifteen years ago, and which now must look like oak trees or a knotted rope; for Mrs. Meredith, who said we all have rhythm, and produced a stethoscope to prove it; let us pray.

For our heart, which lately has felt as if it is skipping beats, which our doctor friend tells us is normal—think of it as resetting itself, he said, like an iPhone; for our heart, which Peter says feels fine when we place his hand to our chest—See? we say, Did you feel that?; for its health; for its steadiness; for the prevention of sudden attacks; for an end to our worries; let us pray.

For our wedding to Peter, which is two months from now, and which we are certain nobody will enjoy; for our grandparents, still living, who have trouble with noise and crowds, and who will definitely be unhappy with the food; for our friend Betsy, who has just been broken up with by Peter's best friend Jonathan, who will also be there; for our brother Jim Junior, who likes alcohol more than he or anyone should; let us pray.

For Jim Junior, all the time; for Jim as a child, who followed us from place to place unceasingly, like a labrador; for Jim at thirteen, his age when we left for college, and his age when our father lost and did not regain his job; for Jim now, too young for his years, too shy, much different than the man we imagined he might one day become when he was young and bright and had springs for limbs; for Jim, who has wrecked two cars in two years; for Jim, who suffered more than we did from the admonitions of our parents; let us pray.

For Jim, our father, and Linda, our mother; for the bright and joyful twosome in the few photographs we have seen of the early years of their marriage; for our father, holding our mother's purse, and our mother, smoking a cigar; for the two of them, dressed in the clothing of the decade prior to our birth, and beaming toward each other with such intimacy that it feels impolite to look; for our mother, whose devotion to the church has increased with age, so that she now goes twice a week; for our father, whose dourness has increased with age, whose church attendance has stopped entirely; let us pray.

For John, the minister at our church when we were growing up; John, for whom we prayed aloud each week (along with a bishop and a presiding bishop whose names we have forgotten, and Ronald Reagan, and Bill Weld, and our sister parish in Harare, Zimbabwe); for John, whose face we pictured when we said our prayers at night; John, who was kind and good and poor and lost his wife and child in a car accident and still loved God; John, whose sermons made us bow our heads in fervent prayer and cry over the number and nature of our childish sins, until we were introduced to the phrase *opiate of the masses* in a freshman survey course at college and stopped going to church except at home, at Christmas; for John, whom our mother says is now eighty-eight years old, and sits in the pews and listens while the new reverend, Pamela, preaches; let us pray.

Poems for Lent

"Deep calleth unto deep at the noise of thy waterfalls: All thy waves and thy billows are gone over me."

— Psalm 42:7

I pray:

may

taking up
what no one
else wants
to carry

become its own
kind of worship

may

faith
become
the substance
of faith

the difference
between air
& water

the world's other body

I kneel down
to diaper it it
laughs to see me
so diapered

•

I put my left ear on the desk
& ask for a poem

nothing arrives
nearby

I put my right ear on my chest
& ask for a poem
where could it be

I make many things
not least among them
errors

I also dream and receive,

That is, the LORD speaketh me:

let us not forget
what is shallow
& what is deep
eventually meet

•

I so often go there
to the damp ground
where it extends its arm
but can't quite
reach

I get on my knees

a stalk in still water
seems to breathe
seems borne of something

genitals cast upon the sea
do not become the seed of beauty
but of deceit

well inside the falls
we break our looking in half
the egg-world in tact
the yoke
darts below
& kills the very last minnow

without wetting me
God there
happens to be

•

I the ode
work furiously

upon fury in each
room of my home

I call out
as stones do
not to You

but to doubt
I love doubt

its firmness
when all else

falls through
it forms

the everlasting
hole

the good news
is this this
selfsame delight

•

the creature
had a tail of water
I loved it loved it loved
it and gave it away

I have a misshapen fever
only another
can calm

him him

he addeth to it
sucking stones
so that I might mouth
something when he goes

that noah built his boat
to rest upon my tongue
means I believe

Father, tell her,
my daughter:
people are not bad
not evil
people want to be like water
and go where currents send them

Post-Game-Day Blessing

Bless the black g-string,
abandoned on the sidewalk
beside a green Gingko
sapling on Lee Street.
Bless the girl who
shimmied out of it
before dawn, drunk
on Curaçao or Triple
Sec or Mike's Hard
Lemonade. Drunk
on lust and early autumn
and our team's unexpected
win over Georgia Tech.
Bless our team, all defense,
no offense. Bless every-
one who must have been
downtown last night
with their car flags and
war whoops, mesh jerseys
and micro-minis. Bless
our star quarterback, on fire
with a 14-3 halftime lead.
We are on the first grade
class walking trip to the
library so everyone can
get their own cards. I am
chaperone, which means
herding kids out of traffic,
back over the curb. Bless
the curb, and the kids who
use it as a balance beam.
Bless the magical book drop.
Bless the girl with knotted

hair who tries to stuff orange
leaves into the slot. And
bless the librarian, too, who
reads a book, loudly, clearly,
to everyone about someone
reading a spooky book. Bless
the meta-story, and the mass
of first graders, descending
on the stacks like locusts.
Bless the red Solo cups
on the return trip
congregating like plastic
flames, like oversized
maraschino cherries on
the early-morning lawns
of Phi Delt, Sig Ep,
any dilapidated white
house with a porch
couch on East Roanoke
Street. Bless the empty
bottles of PBR knocked
on their sides, mouths
open in wondrous O's.
O rushing yards. O Bud
Light Lime in your crushed
cardboard case resting
on the elementary school
lawn. Bless my son and
his friend Major, who look
past the blue Trojan wrapper
on Jackson Street, the flattened
Miller Lite can on Bennett,
to the blue butterfly,
to the giant mushroom
blooming in the corner

of someone's yard. *It looks
like a piece of meat*, says
my son. Or *a tree stump*,
says Major, matter-of-factly.
It is a mushroom worth
blessing. And Bless our team
for escaping Bobby Dodd Stadium
with a 17-10 win. Bless us for
being able to hold on despite
the onslaught.

The Celebration and Blessing of a Marriage

At the time appointed, the persons to be married, with their witnesses, assemble in the church or some other appropriate place.

During their entrance, a hymn, psalm, or anthem may be sung, or instrumental music may be played, as the congregation evaluates the tastefulness of the event and/or stealthily eyes their wristwatches.

Then the Celebrant, facing the people and the persons to be married, addresses the congregation and says

Dearly beloved: We have come together in the presence of God to see for ourselves the marriage of these two people, one a reasonably conscientious and generous person, the other also very much a person, for what it's worth, however much less conscientious or generous. The bond and covenant of marriage was established by people who believed in God, or so the story goes, and demarcates for us the ending of single life and the beginning of a life shared by two or more adults who deeply, let's hope, but at least actually believe that they'll value a relationship defined as a marriage by our church and, probably more importantly, our society.

The union of two or more adults in heart, body, and mind is intended by God for their mutual joy, believe it or not; for the help and comfort given one another in prosperity and adversity, in whatever proportion these two particular people experience such things; and, when it is God's will, for the procreation of children, which, oh boy, will we get to that. Therefore marriage is not to be entered into unadvisedly or lightly, but reverently, deliberately, and only after some ceremonial saying of things, which I now begin.

The Blessing of a Civil Marriage

The Rite begins as the people being married stand before the Celebrant, who addresses them in only and exactly these words

N. and N., you have today found it necessary or suitable to legally and perhaps lovingly become married. In accordance with the proclivities of our particular culture and the prevailing interpretations of various holy texts, I now seek to verify that you each enter into this union intending, with God's grace, to perform the myriad duties and to suffer the requisite frustrations of a typical modern marriage. Okay?

The Celebrant then addresses one of the people being married, saying

N., you are entering into a potentially eternal, but at least life-long, union with N. Do you promise to sustain a more or less positive attitude toward this and all other decisions made by you and your spouse, lest disagreements and regrets interfere with the civility of your shared life? Do you promise to communicate well? Do you promise to address honestly your spouse's concerns, including, for example, the number and nature of the dirtied dishes piled in not one but both sinks in the kitchen, and the sinks relatively deep, too, thus the urgency in your beloved's voice when broaching the subject of just whose turn it is to wash these dishes, which have been compiled by the both of you but which must be washed by just one of you because doing the dishes together really just takes longer and leads to disputes over which methods of washing are most efficient or effective, or, for another example of that about which your spouse might approach you, the frequency and quantity of your drinking? Speaking of which, do you promise to drink only as often and as much as is becoming of a person of your age and in your position in life, taking into account such factors as whether your union here today has yielded children, be they conceived or adopted—consider adoption, it's lovely and fulfilling—anyway, um, so do you promise not to drink so much that you accidentally, in a drunken stupor, diaper your child's head or feed your child half-cooked Buffalo Chicken Wings because you eschewed preparation instructions as much as you eschewed good sense when mixing a fourth screwdriver in an hour, tasty though they may be, both vodka cocktail and raw wing? Seriously, do you promise to manage your tendency to self-medicate the condition I here refer to as thirsty sadness? Do you promise to drink openly, hiding nothing, and to answer your spouse's inquiries and to reply to your spouse's concerns in a levelheaded, considerate way not resembling in the least the kind of angry, self-defensive manner often employed when a person with a problem is confronted by a loved one about that problem, because you realize that having that kid changed everything and you can't be a jerk about these things just because it's inconvenient to face them? Do you know there will be a kid? There's gonna be a kid. Do you promise to envision what sort of human being you'd hope your child could become, and do you promise to aspire to become that sort of human being, despite the undeniable fact that you are far from the sort of person you'd hope anyone would become, to say nothing of your own child, whom you will love more than life itself, which is saying so little that I won't bring further attention to how little it's saying, that you'll love your child more than yourself or your life or the concept of life, that your love for the child will exaggerate grotesquely the distorted, damning image you have of yourself as you try, seemingly in vain though, in truth, with slow progress, to grow into a model for your child you'd like to embody, or at least a model for your child that you don't have to be ashamed of, don't have to berate in boozy, self-recriminatory panic-fests in bed at night next to this person, N., whom today you marry before God and we gathered few? Do you realize that N. is totally gonna rediscover his or her faith when a child hits the scene, a child whose eternal fate N. will experience as so critically important that he or she will return to prayer and, finally, religious devotion to a Heavenly Father you just think he or she doesn't believe in today—because just give that some time; they all come back? Do you know that today you will agree to be wed forever to a person whose worldview will change so profoundly that the two of you will thereafter live in definitively separate worlds while nevertheless remaining bonded by law, and before a God you do not believe in, and will continue to live in the same home, loving and guiding into adulthood the same child? So do you furthermore promise to, you know, suck as little as possible as a person, to remain thoughtful generally, refraining from deleting your spouse's programs from the DVR, for instance, refraining, also, from mocking your spouse's faith in a higher power without which—that faith, that power—your life would actually be worse, would be more hollow, more uncertain, and—can you imagine?—twice as fraught with cosmic fear and eternal loathing, even more spiritually vacant, self-involved, and lonely as it is with just the one of you on the wrong side of conversations concerning God, the soul, and the very dimensions and textures of what it means to be and to be human? Do you promise to be, like, 67% less lazy than you are, with a particular focus on increasing your effort with regard to and investment in—steel yourself here, N.—sex, because not for nothing, decades of being subjected to selfish, inept, merely—and not even always that, as in for everybody—effective lovemaking can make marriage more draining, less rewarding, than it is when each partner actually takes care to cherish the other's body as she or he does that partner's mind, sense of humor, and moral convictions? Do you promise to deal with the inevitable softening and gradual reshaping that all bodies undergo, that your bodies will both undergo as the two of you journey through a life together, becoming more weathered, as does the stone 'neath the water's flow, and exhausted, as do parents, you'll find, with the passage of time? I mean, do you promise to cherish this person at all? Do you promise to remember, forever, why you joined this person here today and had me say all this, to officiate this ceremony and make official this union? Do you have a list, perhaps, of all the qualities you find so charming or however it is you think of who this person is? Do you even know why you're doing this? I mean do you really? Do you think that marrying this person will somehow bring together the far-flung, poorly understood fragments of your life into a shimmering constellation of sense and purpose, that marrying N. will give shape to the amorphous, apparently meaningless mess of your life? Or do you just think that you'll never love anyone else as much as you love N., so you might as well just go ahead and get married, because that's what people do, isn't it, and maybe several years later, after the kid comes into the picture, you'll still feel mostly sure that nobody else would suit you, that you could love nobody else as much, as passionately—and then you'll laugh to yourself at that word, "passion," because of course you are a passionless person, calculating the strength of your love by adding how much you dislike everybody else to how destroyed you'd be able to be if your spouse died, then dividing the sum by how afraid you are of being alone and unloved, all of those being negative factors and the equation yielding a positive, an affirmation: yes, this person now and forever? Do you think of love that way, for goodness sake? Do you know what you're doing, what you're doing to N.?

The first person answers I do.

The Celebrant then addresses the second person, saying

N., do you know what this other person is doing? Do you know what you're doing? Do you still want to do this?

The second person answers I do.

The Celebrant then addresses the congregation, saying

Will you who have come here today to witness the marriage of these two agree that I said some important stuff that N. and N. should really keep in mind before we end this thing? Will you find a balance, helping these two grow and survive without overstepping the bounds of privacy, recognizing and respecting particularly N.'s vague contempt for many of you, the thirsty, sad N. who here eyes our communion wine and licks his or her lips?

People   We will.

The celebrant concludes the ceremony, saying

Bless, O LORD, N. and N., who are doing this no matter what, apparently, and forgive, O LORD, N., for, you know, everything, and reward, O LORD, N., for his or her incredible heart and compassion as these two unite one to the other and vice versa, etcetera, in your grace and glory. Amen.

The Congregation responds   Amen.

For People Who Are Seeing their New Rental for the First Time

Stir up your power, O LORD, and with great might come among us and enter this house. Here it is, this our new house, the one we paid so many thousands of dollars to move to. It is not the house of which we dreamed. O LORD, we feel the press of tears that we cannot allow our family see. Smell it, O LORD! There is a smell of old baking soda rising from this brown carpet, a carpet that stretches from wall to wall, and is for some mysterious reason burnt in two different corners. We imagine what ceremony might have occurred within these walls to bring fire to these rooms and fear that whatever flame appeared herein was burnt not in the celebration of you or in an effort to bring heat to your children in winter, but rather in the service of either creating or ingesting drugs, drugs that might have made the former occupants see visions and feel closer to you but in reality only made them sick and then in need of entering the bathroom. Which, O LORD, is not a room we want to enter. O LORD. We believe, however, in the magic of decoration. We believe in the magic of art. We believe in the magic that our wife has worked on the rooms of all other houses in which we have ever lived, including the one with the mold and roof problems, and sure enough there she is right now, LORD, putting the dining room table in the spot we never would have guessed might work but which is of course the perfect spot. And there is our young daughter, performing a dance that interprets the flight of a leaf caught in the wind. She is dancing her dance across the expansive burnt carpet. "I love the feel of carpet!" she cries, barefoot. "I'm a leaf!" She spins until she collapses under the weight of vertigo only to fight it until she triumphs and rises again. "What do you want me to be now?" she asks, unsteady on her feet, still dizzy but determined. "What? What?" And we say, "A bee." And she says, "A bee rising up through the rain? Rising up through the clouds and into the sunshine?

Where we can't see her but know she is still up there?" "Yes," we say. "Do that dance." And she does that dance, and with her bee we all rise on the updraft of the newness of life, and with her now live and reign not only in this new house and on this burnt carpet but with you, O LORD, above the clouds where we cannot see the bee but have heard from a child here that that is where she is flying. There is a cracked windowpane and a man with a neck tattoo on the curb on the other side of it. He too is now looking up because there has been a clap of thunder. Perhaps he too is a bee. For ever and ever. *Amen.*

For the Unseeable Child in the Rear-Facing Safety Seat

Heavenly Father, relent. Offer stability to our otherwise shaky hands as we attempt to clip our small child into the rear-facing car seat on the passenger side of the car, behind where our spouse would be sitting were this a family trip and not merely a quick ride to daycare. Help us gently fumble with the chubby flesh of our child as she grins and attempts to grab our watch, help us extract the straps through which we then must guide our child's waving limbs, and come to our aid as we seek to make the female and male ends of the two pair of clips fit together as we ourselves fit together with our spouses to make this child we're now so overwhelmingly in love with and so terrified of and for. Father we'll here acknowledge that maybe it's not a trick, maybe it's just the casual, lateral blah blah of a new parent's brain clicking and clanking along, the fact that You never showed Your face to anyone—not Moses in his desert need, not Jacob in his all-night wrestling, not Abraham after he'd cut the binds off Isaac, YHWH here we are trying this weekday morning, Your sky blue and whipped clean of last night's storms, here we are trying to secure this child You've seen fit to grant the biology of our bodies and this child of course LORD is *in your image*. LORD help us. Dear Almighty release the fervent *what if* that clutches like a claw at our soul's throat as we drive down Broadway (not that Broadway) and take a right on Bluffton and a further right on Engle, the dark *what if* every parent lives daily but LORD hear us: this fear is bathed in both blood and spirit. Divine all-knowing, this child we drive (mostly) cautiously while we (mostly) cease checking the phone for an email from nothing, from no one that could possibly be more important or valuable than the health and safety of our progeny, this child that is gift and burden, LORD, not merely burden in that we must awake while we'd rather slumber to soothe this child, in that we have and must and will forever gladly sacrifice

39

for this child whatever resources we've been blessed enough to secure with the work of our hands and bodies nourished by You, but a burden LORD in that this child is *in Your image*, is *of Your spirit*, is (according to cards and grandmotherly strangers) *a gift from You* and LORD there are two train tracks that cross Engle, maybe two hundred yards apart, as you know. At the first we often wait for a slow train as it wheels past and Father there's a grayness of our spirit as the tons of manmade progress and commerce slowly roll along, and we beseech you: what is it? This grayness, this dark inkling that occasionally strikes, all that passes before us? Almighty Everything You know the lengths to which we go to serve you, to deserve to live within such spirit, but LORD sometimes it's fearful, almost intolerable, the attempting to live with grace in the overwhelming everythingness of Your world, trains and the driving of strangers, etc. LORD this child is perfect and each car trip features a pair of worries, the first that harm will befall this child but not us parents, and second that we'd somehow *deserve* that. LORD what we're trying to say is that, at the train tracks, as we wait for the train, sometimes we lean back from the driver's seat, sometimes we lean back and look at the perfect life we've so far not fucked too terribly up or hurt, and that moment, Heavenly Father: that leaned-back glimpse of the rear-facing child's face as we wait for the train to pass, child usually asleep by then, ten minutes in the car, halfway between home and day care, her Cheerios and yogurt and formula as settled in her stomach as they'll get, her chubby hand clutching some plastic thing we don't clean enough. Dear Omnipitent, you know what we mean, know what we began with: summer morning, standing at car's edge, securing our child to an aggregate of machinery that, if it all works as advertised, should be all fine, but then closing the sliding door and driving and traffic, but then not seeing the child's face as she yabbers and chats at the passing trees or whatever, LORD, *faith*, faith is what we seek, grant us faith that all that we're doing is or comes close to being enough to tend the miracles we've been granted custody of in this clumsy, pot-holed world, Holy All-Knowing let us breathe easier as we clip our child into the seat that keeps her face facing away from ours and let us trust that such work (in Your name, always) is *enough*, whatever that term ends up really meaning.

For Gluten

Heavenly father, in your infinite goodness you created the earth and blessed us with its natural bounties, its clear abundant waters and fertile lands yielding plenteous harvests of fruits and vegetables and grains, many of which happen to contain gluten. We praise you, our LORD, for creating gluten, an important yet humble source of worldwide protein enjoyed for centuries by the peoples of many nations, the great majority of whom didn't even know it existed until recently. God, you sent gluten into this world, as you sent your own Son, to save us, not to torment us with vague and possibly imaginary physical symptoms. So please help certain people to remember, gracious LORD, even as they shun and revile gluten, that it is still a creation of your own almighty hand, and that, being God, you maybe knew what you were doing when you created it. Enlighten those among us down here in your flock, O LORD, who go about slandering gluten with great authority and volume although they never heard of gluten until last year. Gently remind these fear-mongering gluten-slanderers to study Wikipedia – which you also created, LORD, so that we might come to know your wisdom more instantaneously – for they might be surprised to learn that gluten was discovered in the 7th century by Buddhist monks who used it as a substitute for meat, thus sparing from slaughter many of your most beloved animals, such as cows, chickens, pigs, and sheep, all of whom might be totally extinct by now were it not for gluten. Also help us to be mindful, O merciful God, of how gluten itself must feel, for who are we to say that gluten does not have feelings? We imagine gluten is appalled, to put it mildly, for as you yourself opined in *Romans* 14.3, "Let not the one who eats despise the one who abstains, and let not the one who abstains pass judgment on the one who eats, for God has welcomed him." Gluten certainly takes no umbrage at the estimated one out of every 135 people who *actually* suffers from celiac disease or

42

the euphemistically yet still hatefully named condition "gluten intolerance." Gluten has been around long enough to know you can't please everyone. No, gluten has no problem with these people. Gluten will tell you who it has a problem with, LORD, and that's the shameless opportunists who have turned "gluten-free" from a legitimate health mandate into a "lifestyle choice" for no reason other than their own personal gain, preying upon the fear and ignorance and vanity of the hitherto gluten-tolerant masses with websites such as Glutenista – "on a mission to Make Gluten-Free Fabulous © for everyone, everywhere" – and the sudden proliferation of such glossy publications as *Gluten-Free Living*, *Simply Gluten-Free*, and *Living Without Magazine* (a self-defeating title if ever we've heard one, since presumably the publishers do not want readers to live without the magazine itself). Gluten knows perfectly well what it says in Exodus 14:14, "The LORD will fight for you, and you have only to be silent," but gluten *has* been silent for centuries and guess what, God, it's not working. Therefore, gracious LORD, gluten would like you to know that it has recently met with an attorney regarding a potential defamation claim. And gluten will tell you something else right now, LORD: It was here long before these gluten-haters were born, and it will be here long after they're gone. Not unlike yourself, O LORD, gluten is here to stay.

For the Good and Proper Use of Money

Almighty God, we ask a blessing upon our daily financial trans-
actions, that we might use our money wisely and with vigilant
eyes keep good records of its comings and goings, because the
truth is we aren't that great with keeping track and furthermore
we humbly ask forgiveness for having never learned—or, to be
perfectly honest, having never exhibited the necessary interest
or effort or the required willpower—to appropriately manage
the modest, albeit more than sufficient, capital that comes into
our possession each month. Forgive us for having failed to construct or even consider a clear strategy for long term financial
viability, for having not bothered to invest in or learn about the
stock market, at least not beyond the conservatively diversified
portfolio provided to us by the institution that controls our
employer's investments, and though we have considered creating more aggressive stock market strategies, we know this will
involve scheduling a session with a representative from Human
Resources, an event that would most likely break up our work
day in an inconvenient way, not to mention that we will be
asked to scrutinize a subject we'd rather not think about, i.e.,
our finances, which would mean that the subject of our forty
thousand dollars worth of student loans will be brought up by
an advisor who will tell us that we need to be more proactive
about reducing our debt, and that we should immediately create a family budget to better organize our finances, a suggestion
that would seem, as it always has, absolutely necessary, even
if we've subsequently ignored every one of the family budgets
that we've drawn up over the years, in part because when we
inventory the amount of income we can expect every month
and all of the various directions we can expect the money to go,
it always seems like even if we overestimate the various averages
(like entering a thousand a month for food, which is of course
outrageous), that we have hundreds of dollars left over, but,
then again, we always forgetting that whenever we get ahead,

a car battery needs to be replaced and the piano needs to be tuned and our children's soccer dues need to be paid and we have a wedding to attend which means we have to pay for gas and food and lodging and the dog will have to stay at a dog hotel and so-and-so's birthday is next week and wouldn't it be nice to give a gift card to the beloved music teacher at school and this list could go on and on as the money-separating events keep coming and every month our family breaks basically break even but instead of doing anything about it, the pattern continues, simply because our approach to the family finances basically amounts to "We don't like to think about that so we won't," and so, for the most part, we fail to keep track of the checks we write or the purchases we make via check card, have not written a single number or description in the cell of a check registry for more than a decade, and even back we'd kept shoddy records at best, and thus ended up becoming the kind of people who preferred to basically just not know how much money we actually have, because if we didn't know we won't worry and not worrying about stuff is high on our list of priorities—in fact, if there was one thing you could say about us it's that we appear to live our lives free of worry, a state of mind that we maintain in part by crumpling ATM receipts before we can glance at the balance and, yes, this is not a responsible way to live and, yes, we understand that this is a position of privilege and, yes, we often feel badly about all the money we have, over the course of our lives, wasted on cups of coffee and snacks and expensive beer and how we have often felt entitled to order a double and then another double or the best or the biggest or the most expensive entrée a restaurant offered, a people who, if we were to find something we liked on eBay or Amazon were likely to say, "We'll take it," who, if we had any extra, we spent it, either because we might as well or because we were obliged, but who also liked to think that had someone in need asked us for money, we would have given them some, supposing we had any to give, which we often do, and if for some reason we didn't, we would

45

certainly find a way to help that somebody out—at least that's what we like to think, because we like to imagine ourselves as a people who could not be said to care very much—if at all—about money, and so LORD, we ask thee to bless what we have, and may what little that is take root and grow, in Your holy Name.

For Lost Phones

Oh LORD, apotheosis of infinite creative capabilities, ur-master of highest-def functionality, extreme initiator of the ever-responsive user experience that is our humble life upon Thine Earth, which we rate seven stars on a scale of one to five upon Celestial Yelp, let us pray for all tools we have forged to enhance our UX on Earth. Let us acknowledge the simple spade with which we once dug into Thine Earth. Let us smile upon the common harrow with which we once performed long-forgotten agrarian tasks. Let us bask in a warm streaming downpour of gelatinous joyous bliss regarding the proliferation of electronics, from obsolete switchboards to novel hyperdynamic thermonuclear wristwatches, all of which are no more than tools with which we optimize our UX upon Thine Earth, although some of which are more difficult to concoct and require otherworldly inspiration, unearthly patience, and a zillion hours of terrestrial expertise. Oh LORD, let us now marvel at today's intelligent telephones. Their complexity pales only when compared to the mind-melting macrocosmic design inherent in everything from the tiniest particles on Thine Earth to the farthest flung flouncy interstellar stuff at the edge of Thine awesome universe. Oh LORD, let us now acknowledge how addictive are Thine smart phones, without which we would be ignorant of the weather and our GPS coordinates, without which we would not be able to transmit photos of Thine good Earth across its breadth in an instant. Oh LORD, let us not forget the many apps, the innumerable apps. Oh LORD, is the iPhone itself nothing less than an ark with an app for every animal aboard it? Is the iPhone itself not an ark on which we float upon a flood of info unleashed to confuse those without dedicated wireless access? LORD, let us pray today for those who lose their phones, who therefore cannot instantaneously text an image of their cherubically cute little child to that child's grandparents. Let us pray for those who lose their phones and therefore cannot follow character-restricted utterances regarding occurrences on far-flung fields of play. Let us pray, dear LORD, for those whose phones are not with them today, and yet they suffer phantom rings upon their thighs and fight temptation every fifteen minutes to check for electronic transmissions or blog updates regarding their favorite professional football teams. Oh LORD, let us pray that those whose phones have been lost look around them and recognize that Thee produced a world one must not forsake in favor of character-restricted excrescences rarely attempting to relate its ineffable awesomeness, seven mega-pixel reductions of its organic 360° surround-sound 3D glories. The posture, too, oh LORD, really concerns us. Forgive us, dear LORD, most upright citizen of every corner of the universe, for slouching over phones in public. Forgive us for slouching over phones while walking upon Thine sidewalks, unaware of oncoming pedestrians and Thine glories all around. Let us pray, oh LORD, that those who lose their phones are no longer lost. Let those without phones be a shining light, a beacon, a model for future righteous action, oh LORD, for all who each day willfully exchange Thine world of infinite super-def riches for immersion in the comparably pitiful fraction of it found within their so-called smart phones.

For Post-Interview Job Candidates

O Father of knowledge, he who knows all, including exactly what the University of Eastern Oregon has already decided in regard to who they plan to hire, please tell them to pick us and to let us know that they have done so right away. Because we have moved four times in four years and we have a four-year-old daughter and we do not want to make her move again, because at night recently, before she falls asleep, she has begun telling us how much she misses our old neighbors in Wyoming, which is the last state we lived in, and the whole time we had been telling ourselves she was too young to even miss anything yet, that she wouldn't ever even remember Wyoming, but now we realize that she not only remembers the state, but she even re-members the names of the neighbors' cats, Milo and Satchmo, and the nicknames of the trees in our yard, Big Mamma and Big Sister, and most of all she remembers Beth, the nine-year-old who lived next door and would come over and play dress up and baby doll with our daughter for hours and make her feel special and loved and like she had a big sister, which she does not. And now she no longer has Beth, or any new neighbors who can even take Beth's place, because the neighbors here are mostly older and their children have all left for college and the ones next door are not only old and a little weird but they're super religious (sorry, LORD) and put antiabortion posters in their yard (Sorry again, but you know what we mean). But if the University of Eastern Oregon picks us, we will buy a house there and stop moving and at least have a chance to find a new Beth, one we might know for more than just one cycle of sea-sons. And if they don't pick us, we're going to move again, for another year, and we don't want to do that. And it's after five o'clock, which is when they said they would let the job final-ists know what they've decided, and we've been refreshing our email inbox all day and are actually holding our cell phone in our hand right now, in case it rings or vibrates which we might

49

not otherwise hear or feel if it was only sitting on the table or in our pocket. Dear LORD, please enable this cell phone to ring, enable our inbox to receive an email, enable us to receive this news without incident. In fact, if you could just enable the news to come at all, that would be good. Even if it's bad. Any news will help, because now it's even later, and our left eyelid has begun to twitch and we're afraid to go home and tell our wife and daughter that it isn't even that we do or don't have the job, it's that we still don't even know and that we all have to keep waiting. And we have to move out of this house in five weeks regardless. So enable the news to come. You know what they've decided. You know what they're going to do. Let us know, oh LORD, and really, if you can make them pick us we will stop tearing up those weird posters next door. We'll leave them standing there in the crabgrass for as long as they might last. Ah! The phone is ringing! We're looking at it, closely. It isn't the University of Eastern Oregon. It's our wife. Through Jesus Christ our LORD. *Amen.*

For the Harmless Yet Disgusting Parasitic Nematodes That Last Week Briefly Infected Our Children

O God, the Father of all, in whose kingdom live all manner of creature, disgusting and beautiful alike, rid us of this most recent blight that has infected our bed sheets, our pillows, our carpets, and the bodies of our children.

As we sit on our couches each evening, LORD, longing for a respite from days of our children's tears and whining, our snapping, our judgment, and we listen not to the soothing sounds of *Breaking Bad* reruns or *Monday Night Football*, but instead to our children whimpering in their sleep, grant us peace. Grant us peace that we might sleep, LORD. Prevent this nematode, this parasite whose only purpose in life is to consume and procreate (and are we, after all, so different, LORD?), commonly called the pinworm, from emerging out of the rectums of our children to lay its eggs. In its way this is a natural process, a beautiful one, even, in that it is a further example of life and death and of your infinite kingdom. But, LORD, forgive us, the pinworm is gross.

We know, LORD of Mercy, that infection of this particular parasite has no socio-economic significance; neither is it, God of Light and Power, a sign of uncleanliness, but for this reason, we ask that you rid us of this worm for there is nothing quite like an itchy ass caused by a nearly microscopic worm, to make those of us who are fathers and mothers of children with these itchy asses feel like failures as parents. We worry we have failed, O God, to properly cleanse and disinfect our children. We worry that we have failed in other, graver ways, too. We worry we have failed to keep our children safe and healthy, and that this simple failure is promise of those much larger to come.

Did you worry about this, O LORD? About your Son and the way His earthly parents cared for Him? Grant us mercy and grace, Almighty, because we worry about this constantly. We watch our children sleep, LORD, we watch them on the playground, eat dinner, wrestle and play with each other, and perform the simplest of tasks, and we think, O God, we think: have we done this right? Is there some vital skill we have failed to give them? Are we creating monsters? Is the damage already done, silently growing inside them until adulthood? Is it all our fault?

It's the small stuff that stings hardest, God. Look graciously upon us as we trudge forward in our parenthood. Cleanse our children of all parasites, allow the worms to pass harmlessly from our children's bodies. Likewise, cleanse our children of our bad advice, grant them protection from our bad decisions, from our blundering, and our fears. Keep them safe from all dangers, most of all those that we blindly and unknowingly place in their paths. Give us the strength, Everliving God, to make the midnight drive to Walgreen's for medicine to cure our children. Let us not be overcome with annoyance when that Walgreen's doesn't have what we need. Grant us always the wisdom to drive to the other Walgreen's and purchase the medicine, and let this be a symbol for our parenting. Until our children are old enough, and even beyond, keep us from failure, let not our idiocy and calamity injure our children, O LORD. In the name of your Son, the Prince of Peace and Clean Bodies, we pray. *Amen.*

For the Spudnuts, As They Take to the Sky

Dear LORD, bless us here, in Arco, as our air quality gets the
Green Square every time, which means Good, if not God, if
not You. Our air is good here. Thanks for that. We like to
breathe, and we breathe easy. We trap in our spudnuts this air,
and this air, like the river, finds its path of least resistance, and
builds channels through the dough—the potato, the egg, the
sugar, the flour, the salt. Though slick with oil, it is this Green
Square air that keeps our spudnuts light, our Good godly potatoes that allow for the combative density. LORD, You know: in
the spudnut, is argument between one good thing that wants
to ground us, and another that wants to lift us from this earth.

•

Here, our famous tuber oozes the sort of starch we can dress
only in confectioner's sugar, and a quick dip in the magma of
our morning coffee. Forgive us our idols...

•

Bless this black earth. This earth is (according to the Craters of
the Moon National Monument brochure we keep under our
pillows like a tooth, keep under our pillows as if waking to
it is waking to reward, and a breakfast at Pickle's Place of egg
and hash browns, and the kind of spudnut so ephemeral we
swear we lift for a moment from our seats and hover here in
this Good air, a lovely half-inch of it now separating our blue
jeans from the seat cushion [also black], which makes us think
of the sky and the bearded men who live in it, and all of the
scorched earth beneath it, of how *scorched* here means Good
Quality and Downright Breathable, and today even, high on
our state's famed potato doughnuts, Otherworldly, and Fifth
Largest Satellite of the Solar System) A *Violent Past, Calm Present, and Uncertain Future*... We finish our breakfast. We beseech
our brochure—false prophet. We will walk off the third spudnut
on the exact earth on which You, Dear LORD, compel the
astronauts to practice for their moon landings. Here, it's right

up the road.

•

Here, a conduit is a vent, and a vent is our passage from crust to core, and core is where we beg Your mercy. We can traverse this with our mouths, find that nothing else lives at the center of the spudnut, but spudnut itself.

•

Forgive also our uncles who complain that there's nothing special about a doughnut made with potato flour, in spite of our uncles being with the Idaho Potato Commission since its inception in 1937. They say there's nothing special about putting the potato on the radio, on television, on the license plate, on T-shirts and underpants and postcards and keychains and mugs, on forearms via tattoo, and in dreams via the 14-hour workday. Nothing special about the potato at trade shows, a Board of Directors of the Idaho Potato, and Frequently Asked Questions that include What Makes Idaho Potatoes So Good? and Why Are My Potatoes Turning Green? We honor You in breathing in this Good Green Air, and answer our uncles' complaints with the slogan on our own blessed sweaters, "Changing the world, one Spudnut at a time." In the sweetening of the starch that is our birthright, we can both engage and manipulate the potato. Look graciously upon us, as we say, *It is ours. It is above us. It is air, moon, the sort of birthright that greens when exhumed from the soil and bathed in sun, like a tree.*

•

Save us from our uncles who say, *Fuck Craters of the Moon, they blew off the bombs there.* Right or wrong, it is the landscape on earth that most closely resembles that of the moon. We wonder how many spudnuts we'd have to eat to uncouple from this soil, our skin greening—so alien!—the higher we rise.

•

Look with pity upon us as we ascend, as we explore *this weird and scenic landscape.* Here, even our brochures think we're odd.

•

54

As if talisman, medical mask, the only thing they know, our uncles hold spudnuts to their faces when stepping outside. We wonder about the quality of that air. Hear us: we wonder what color is even better than Green.

•

Watch over Signature Spudnut, manufacturer of Spudnut™ Mix, as they claim that the ideal spudnut should be "so airy, it seems to float." Here, the rising from this earth is not a move toward death, but an ideal in life, in the starchiest of prayers, and in breakfast. Sure, we have this lovely black earth, but that air—that air which we can take inside of us, but still can't quite reach—is Green, and therefore, both the luminous color of alien skin, and edenic.

•

Grant us the strength to finish the August 2007 article in *The Telegraph*, in which the physicists decided, "levitation has been elevated from being pure science fiction to science fact." Said physicists cited a law called the Casimir Force, a consequence of quantum mechanics that works on the principles of repulsion— a "free" object being repelled by the very surface that should seem to embrace it. In principle, these physicists declare, this "effect could be used to levitate bigger objects... even a person." We wonder about the fluctuations in the energy field of the spudnut, those lovely chambers of air between the soft caves of potato, stretched like the sort of cotton candy that lifts into the air with each exhale, communing with the molecules of Arco, and beyond that, two kinds of moon.

•

The earth, our uncles say in unison, will toss us from its surface like pop-flies.

•

Have pity on the town of Arco, as it was originally called Root Hog, was named for Georg von Arco, a visiting German physicist of radio transmission who invented radio vacuum tubes, which, among other things, found a way to levitate information, the human voice now airborne, disseminating important messages from our home-state about things like atomic power, floating lava fields, and when, exactly, a baked potato is "done."

•

O LORD, You know: that Arco was the first city in the world (in 1955) to be lit by atomic power is obvious. That, up until recently, one was able to buy non-weapons-grade plutonium right next to the Regular Unleaded at Dave's Travel Plaza on the US-20 (which also peddles some of the best spudnuts in town), less so.

•

Here, the spudnut, like the split atom, is inevitable. We wonder which will allow us to levitate first.

•

How much, LORD, of our body is comprised of voice? Guide us among the crater-field of our earthly concerns: If von Arco found a way for our voices to float and fly, will the body follow, as if a dog on a leash? We hold our arms out to our sides. We stand on our toes. Our skeletons, ever clunky, remain earthbound. But when we shout, we are airborne.

•

When we broadcast our voices to others—to so many at once— we are *on air*.

•

Forgive us our fearful uncles who no longer fish in the Big Lost River, which, in spite of its proximity to the nuclear reactor testing station, has remarkably clean waters. As ever, the moon keeps quiet on this, so bless us, Dear LORD, finally, with Your most lunar of voices.

•

Our uncles say they are losing themselves. On our knees, we can wonder if loss is just another kind of levitation.

•

Save us from our scientists who, down the street from Craters of the Moon, at the Idaho National Laboratory, use that non-weapons-grade plutonium to produce levels of heat and electricity sufficient to rocket the vessel (cheesily-named *New Horizons*) into deep space toward the dwarf planet Pluto. Watch over us, and the men and women down the street, who eat spudnuts on Sundays, who breathe the same atomic Green air that we do, who launched that vessel from the earth with the greatest-ever speed for a man-made object. If something leaves the earth so fast, it's *fastest-ever*, we wonder to what degree desire is involved. We wonder about the heart of the atom, and if it's the collection of these atomic hearts, rather than our own dumb four-chambered one, that's responsible for our love of the dough-nut, for our fingering of our great-grandmothers' opal wedding rings in the right pockets of our blue jeans.

•

Guide us as we remember our uncles fishing for trout called bull and trout called rainbow and trout called cutthroat. As we wonder how a name of a thing affects its flavor. As we wonder how the spudnut can taste so good.

•

Here, buoyancy has little to do with water, more to do with the kind of lava we can walk on. In this, we sense a holy act, wonder about the intersection of the mystic and the geologic. Dupe us, please God, again and again...

•

Enable us to see the universe as something other than a deep fat fryer...

•

Compel our legs. We walk to the corner of Front and Temple, to the giant green rocking chair in front of Pickle's Place, from which, as children, even after baskets of spudnuts, we used to leap, counting the seconds we were airborne before landing in the dust, silently beseeching You.

•

In her own prayer-state, St. Teresa of Avila was said to levitate. "I confess that it threw me into a great fear," she writes, "for in seeing one's body thus lifted up from the earth… (and that with great sweetness if unresisted) the senses are not lost; my body seemed frequently to be buoyant, as if all weight had departed from it." Go easy on her. She's a saint, after all.

•

Dear LORD, let us be like Teresa, even as we wonder if levitation is merely an emotional state. Even as we wonder this as we hike and hike on the hardened tephra of Craters of the Moon, the airfall material ejected by a volcano, now keeping us aloft and, for the time being, upright.

•

When *New Horizons* was launched in January 2006, were You watching over us, divining our futures, as we, and our uncles, and our then-new girlfriends celebrated with warm spudnuts from Dave's? That April, as we celebrated our six-month anniversaries with kisses and spudnuts, *New Horizons* bypassed Mars, and our uncles complained, watching reruns of "Deep Space Nine," that they could "retire from the potato, but the potato couldn't retire from us." Ten months later, they mutter about the potato as planet, as shackle, as dependency, parasite, as a right cursed and a right God-given. Have mercy on our uncles—they say nothing of orbits, or of letting-go, but they've stopped watching television, staring instead at the wall, if only because the wall (they say) is a larger screen. Our girlfriends kiss potato from our mouths. Our Ford Windstars are in the shop. Craters of the Moon is too far to walk to. We stare at the blank sheetrock and speculate on our uncles' powers of projection. God bless *New Horizons* as it passes Jupiter.

•

And bless also, LORD, the Ch'an monk, Ying-fung, if only because he levitated (as did his master Nan-chuan). In the year 621, he performed this feat over battlefields during the Battle of Hulao in order to distract the warring soldiers from their fight. But You know this already. You know that our uncles, without breaking eye contact with the wall, whisper to our concerned girlfriends about a whirlpool on Mars over which rocks and (purportedly) humans can levitate. Allow us the heart to tell them: *New Horizons* passed Mars over a year ago.

•

Redeem our uncles who are becoming increasingly insomniac, who wonder if we're misguided when we associate *falling* with *asleep*, *up* with the waking, as if both were directionally bound to a single vertical axis. As if both, like the Big Lost, didn't meander as a rule.

•

Look graciously upon the team of physicists that used the Casimir Force to explain levitation, and who earlier deduced that the "invisibility cloak" is a feasible creation, and that we should have a prototype within twenty years.

•

Forgive and untangle St. Joseph of Copertino, who, riding an air we imagine as even Greener than Idaho's, as pillowy at least as The Best Spudnut in Town, levitated so aggressively in the 17th century that he became entangled in the branches of an olive tree, and refused to come down, even when the Pope brought a ladder and demanded that he shed some of this lofty ecstasy. Copertino levitated so often and effortlessly, that it took on an air of braggadocio, and the Pope therefore, as punishment for the insubordination of allowing a miracle to become commonplace (*there's fucking Copertino levitating again...*) banned Copertino from attending public services for 35 years.

•

Enable us to see that locked in the spudnut is the power of banishment. That it's all we can do to release it with our teeth, swallow the atomic burst of sweet-salty air before it rides away from us at launch speed.

•

In the spudnut is our endurance of time on this earth, is our compulsion to name our own phenomena after that of the moon's, is our awareness of a loftier other-side that's both invisible, and greener.

•

Watch over the sighing spudnut. The potato, says the Idaho Potato Commission, is the "aristocrat in burlap," ever giving a "dependable performance." We breathe in its steam, kiss our girlfriends with stately mouths. Like a mosquito confessing in our ears, The Idaho Department of Environmental Quality cloaks its obviousness in a seductive whisper, and says, "Air is basic to life."

•

We wonder how the volcano can be both explosive and basic. Wonder about a time when, in Idaho, these firestorms came from below us, lifted us up to the sort of place where we can build a place like Pickle's, and the sort of plant that launches a vessel that takes such a long time to get where it's going, even as it's the fastest of its kind.

•

Sienese nuns levitate, and St. Adolphuses levitate, and Zulu sangomas levitate, as do Iranian dervishes, Brazilian mediums, legless lamas, well-hung fakirs, and guys named Padre Pio. Enable them to come down to us. We assume that in ascension is ascension to a better place. In Idaho, Better Place is measurable by Color, Quality, and the powdered sugar of Fugitive Dust and Regional Haze.

•

Our Better Place is in the particulates.

•

Light levitates. Our girlfriends juggle their spudnuts. Make our girlfriends as good as the air. Enable them to never touch the earth.

•

 Forgive our wariness of the fryolator, which, like the volcano, is "a serious fire risk."

•

The spudnut connects our dirt to our sky. Conduit, vent... We can only wonder which is moving toward which. We can only pull our floating spudnuts from the grease, and hope to find the path to You.

•

Our Uncles, choral, have their first heart attacks as *New Horizons* passes Saturn. Their fourth as it passes Uranus. On July 14, 2015, the estimated date when the vessel will finally reach Pluto, save us from the fate of our uncles as they claim they will return "to the atoms of this fucking town," by which we'd like to believe they mean that they will be the ones to illuminate the street lanterns for the first time again, the residents lining Main Street and clapping in what used to be, given the volcanic earth, one of the darkest nights on the populated planet.

•

Above us, the moon quakes like the earth. Still our hearts, LORD, in the shockwave wake. There are Venusquakes and Marsquakes and sunquakes and starquakes. Among other things, astronomers call these "sudden adjustments." In the tent at the Craters of the Moon campground, overlooking Inferno Cone and Echo Crater, The Monoliths and Devil's Orchard, and the cinders and The Cinders, post-coital, we think nothing of the roiling heat of the cooking oil, the way the spudnut repeats its exhale with each of our subsequent bites, the potato as pillar and idol and fruit fallen to lava, and our girlfriends shudder in their mummy bags and we wonder if they're really that cold, or imitating Andromeda as they shift, suddenly, in sleep.

•

...and all the world goes Good Green, and Big Lost.

•

...a little airborne...

•

Make of *New Horizons* a universal alarm clock. The spudnut as the act waking, and the act of waking, down, or left.

•

The internal composition of the moon includes a core that's

three times smaller than that of the average terrestrial body. Forgive its smallness. *Blessed are the meek...* It has to beat thrice as hard for the moon to maintain its composure.

•

You know, LORD Almighty: there's something about the night at Craters of the Moon that invites the stuff inside us to shift like those mechanical wave machines, tipping its dye-blue liquid to one wall and then another. We wonder—Bless us!—if that fluttery stuff can ever escape, ride some shaft of air up and out of our mouths, bury itself, for just a moment, in the spongy crumb of the spudnut, before rising again from it. You know, LORD, our God-Yahweh-Adonai: we're so far out into the earth here—there's nothing lit like the lamps of Arco. Here, we can't tell where the earth stops and the sky begins; those stars over there could be littering the rocks upon which the astronauts practice. So preserve our bodies as we listen to The Best of Holly Cole on a tiny battery-operated radio in the tent, and as she sings her syrupy version of "I Can See Clearly Now," throws it, as if, all the way to Pluto, or some other decade-long journey, we think nothing of von Arco, and his radio, the wall our uncles watch while massaging their own chests, the static they listen to on the transistor for messages between the noise, and the stuff inside us shifts. At first, we think, this means we are going to throw up, that we've eaten, if it's possible, too many spudnuts, until, in zombie-daze, with Your guidance, O LORD, we unzip the canvas, walk to the Windstars, the pitch-dark meat in some celestial sandwich, and retrieve our Great-Grandma Sarah's opal rings from the backpacks. Allow us to be men both aristocratic and dependable. Allow us to be the kind of intersection at which kids fly from a big green chair.

•

Bless us with the knowledge that here, levitation is just another kind of proposal.

•

Even now, our girlfriends mutter potato names in their sleep—

Lady, Amandine, Russet, Snowden, Pink-eye, Megachip, Marcy, Golden, and Idaho, and Idaho as if naming children or dogs, as if calling in tongues, from the basement carpet of dream, to our satellites and projectiles, and to You, and to everything over our heads—even those slippery uncaught trout swimming backfirst in a chamber of riverwater both nuclear and pristine, their own tongues channeling the last orgasm of Ying-fung. Bless us even now, when we know what we are supposed to do, but can't rule out vomiting, the stars, and the potatoes beneath them nudging us in a very precise, but appropriately aeriform direction, that, given the physics of this love, feels decidedly upward, even as we fall and fall.

For the Woman Who Bought a Groupon...

...for the service of not one but three Brazilian waxes—the fact she had never before had a Brazilian notwithstanding, as she had for many years regularly subjected herself to the pain and humiliation of standard bikini waxing and so stupidly thought, How much worse can it be?—because, budget being an issue, it seemed to the woman a wise and thrifty thing to do (the package rate of three Brazilians proving considerably less expensive than a single standard bikini wax purchased at full price three times—she'd done the math), not to mention the woman's regular girl (did she really just call someone her girl?) had recently decided to abandon her career at the day spa in hopes of completing a degree in taxidermy, thus leaving the woman in search of a new girl (there she goes again) and what better opportunity to give a girl a cosmetologist a try-out than at a discounted rate, and furthermore the woman thought, having been married now for over a decade, Why not spice things up? (a notion lifted straight from the glossy pages of MORE magazine); and whose babysitter twenty minutes before the Brazilian appointment cancelled via text message, thereby placing the woman in a bit of a conundrum for she had promised to take her children to the pool this afternoon and, not wanting to shave her bikini line in order to do so (as that would require waiting another couple of weeks for the hair to grow long enough to be effectively waxed, by which time the first of the three Groupons will have expired), the woman briefly considered postponing the appointment merely a day or two and proceeding to the pool without shaving—a scenario in which she would be obliged to keep her shorts on and therefore stay out of the water on this the hottest day of the year while her children would, no doubt, loudly and repeatedly while tugging on her limbs, beg the woman to get in the pool and play with them, and in so doing would attract the attention of the other mothers—the ones in their floppy twill hats, the ones who would be so thickly slathered in non-toxic, oxybenzone-free sunscreen that it shows greasy white across their shoulders, the ones who joyfully splash around with their children every day as if there is absolutely nothing on earth they'd rather be doing, the ones whose swimsuits look like dresses and who probably ceased any sort of grooming down there long ago (if, in fact, they ever bothered with such nonsense for this is a town crammed to the gills with bushy eye-browed La Leche League militants) and who would, every one of them, be listening for the woman to offer an acceptable reason for refusing to play in the pool with her children, a thing for which these mothers have already determined there is no acceptable reason—and so it was with this in mind the woman made the snap and ill-conceived decision to keep the Brazilian appointment and take her children along, hence filling their backpacks with snacks and coloring books and Hotwheels and Polly Pockets, and charging them to keep busy and quiet while mommy gets...a massage, and once she had situated the children on a magenta chaise in the salon's waiting area, and after half-heartedly assuring the fabulous gay receptionist that her progeny would be no trouble at all, the woman followed the new girl, Misty, into her assigned chamber and, as instructed by Misty, stripped from the waist down, draped herself with the Egyptian cotton towel provided, and climbed onto the padded table where she now lies—knees in the air, eyes on the paisley wallpapered ceiling, Misty between her legs—enduring a procedure about which the answer to the question: How much worse can it be? is becoming clearer by the second, clearer with each time Misty meticulously applies a strip of searing hot wax, waits for it to harden, then rips it off saying: Exhale, when she has never bothered to say: Inhale, and it is at one of these such excruciating moments the woman realizes that, in her haste to be punctual, she has forgotten to take the preemptive dose of Vicodin (left over from her C-section) as her babysitter had advised—the same babysitter who cancelled, the babysitter who is a hairless blonde waif—but it is too late now, the torture is

65

well underway, as Misty manipulates the woman into various awkward positions in order to gain leverage at different angles, all the while gabbing gabbing gabbing, and ripping, and saying: Exhale, and gabbing some more, gabbing about where in town to get the best fish taco, gabbing about the prejudicial scoring at her son's skateboard tournament, gabbing about the Kardashians and the hoarders and the twerking, pausing every so often to look expectantly at the woman, who remains silent, not only because she has nothing to contribute to this vapid conversation, but because at this point (Rip! Exhale!) she would surely be unable to speak without weeping, and THEN, just as she (the Groupon woman) thinks things could not get any worse, the restless voices of her children begin to penetrate the chamber walls (Luke Skywalker this, Kit Kittredge that) and the woman asks how much longer and Misty says only half done and the woman says how can such a small area take so much time and Misty says I'm a perfectionist and the woman says my lucky day and THEN, as the woman hears the unmistakable zip of Hotwheels racing across travertine tile and consequently begins to reevaluate her No Electronics parenting philosophy, Misty asks would she like a landing strip or a heart shape or possibly a monogram(!) and in response, the woman, confused, explains to Misty that she had understood a Brazilian by definition to mean the whole ball of wax, the whole she-bang as it were, thusly cracking herself up—these idioms! in this situation!—but Misty is blank, she doesn't get it (though to be perfectly fair: Misty doesn't get much) and whereas the children's voices are growing louder and louder with phrases like how does that work and what's this thing for, the woman—left knee next to her ear, heel flexed toward the ceiling, foot tingling with the urge to kick Misty in the face (at which point Misty actually says: Don't kick me, as if she could read the woman's mind)—continues to crack up in spite of herself, and THEN from outside the chamber comes a terrible crash, and everything falls silent, except Misty who keeps gabbing about vajazzle and pedazzle and pelvic tattoos, and as she (Misty) tweezes and chips at stubborn bits of hardened wax, a lone hot tear escapes the woman's eye, rolls down her temple and into her ear canal, and she is certain that when this is over she will be so apologetic that she will give to the fabulous gay receptionist (who must think she's from hell, which makes the woman very sad because gay men used to adore her and, let's face it, there is no higher compliment) a gratuity twice the amount of the service itself, never to return, thereby forfeiting the two remaining Groupons and resuming her search for a new girl who is more like her old girl (the future taxidermist), a girl who will not speak, will not utter a single word as she works, but will loop a lovely playlist of new age harps and Native American flutes, overdubbed with the sound of ocean waves and distant thunder, while she manicures for the woman in this tranquil setting a nice, natural triangle, neat and trim, the kind to which the woman has become accustomed, and about which, by the way, her husband has never had any complaints, and equipped with which she may wear a sexy-yet-tastefully-age-appropriate bikini and enjoy the simple pleasure of lying in the sun, freed from concern for the unseemly exposure of androgenic hair; but who, for now, lies in pain and humiliation beneath paisley wallpaper, helpless to the perfectionism of Misty who says, again too late, Exhale!

We beseech thee, O gracious LORD, have mercy.

For a Teenage Girl Embarking Upon a Week-long Carnival Cruise with Her Parents

O most omniscient God our Father, Who art everywhere, even upon the high seas, look with mercy upon fifteen-year-old Deena Truitt as she sets sail with her parents on a week-long cruise on the Carnival Breeze, departing from Miami, Florida in August with three ports of call in the exotic Caribbean and an all-inclusive holiday package featuring a variety of exciting onboard entertainment, non-stop luxury dining, fun-filled youth programs, whale and dolphin viewing, and much, much more. Help Deena not to lose her sense of breathless anticipation as she stands in an interminably long line in a vast and overcrowded embarkation hall with her father, Bob Truitt (flowered shirt, khaki shorts, reddish hair, and sunglasses), and her mother, Barbara Truitt (turquoise blouse, white stretch slacks, sensible shoes, and a lightweight metal quad cane), together with their definitely-not-luxurious mob of fellow travellers who have come provisioned with ice chests of beer, novelty foam hats, and boomboxes. Remind her, dear LORD, as her parents will also, that Bob and Barbara have been planning and saving for this cruise for three years, and it may be the last chance they'll get to spend this much time together as a family, what with their little girl starting high school already, and Barbara's bad knees, and who-knows-what's-going-to-happen with Bob's position at Sears, now with the cutbacks and layoffs. Let them enjoy their well-deserved Caribbean cruise vacation. Let them get their money's worth.

Hover over Deena, ever-present LORD, in the tiny, portholed stateroom she shares with her parents, the one that smells suspiciously of spray disinfectant and sewerage; assist her in repositioning her cot as far away as possible from her father, who snores. And later that afternoon, at the Sail Away Party on the Lido Deck, when Butch the cruise director coaxes Deena's father into joining the Hairy Chest Competition, and

Bob, although he doesn't win (he doesn't stand a chance, not with his pale flabby torso), nevertheless jumps enthusiastically into the Back It Up line dance, where Butch, wild-faced and hooting, slaps him repeatedly on the butt, shouting, "Hump it, Mr. Man! Hump it hard!": do Your best to restrain Deena from flinging herself over the nearest rail into the sea. For this is her father, and these are her parents, and no matter how utterly grotesque they appear to her, she knows she must continue to abide with them, at least for another week.

Follow Deena, vigilant LORD, when she disembarks with her parents at their first port of call on the isle of Grand Turk, an enchanting colonial paradise complete with olden-style British pubs, working windmills, picture-perfect beaches, and always-smiling and friendly islanders. Try not to lose sight of her when, in an attempt to distance herself from her parents, she foolishly wanders off by herself up the beach, away from the well-scrubbed Carnival Cruise Complex, turns inland, and soon finds herself in an unpaved warren of cinderblock homes with dirty bed sheets for doors, and starved, mangy-looking dogs nosing in piles of garbage. Confer with Deena, O LORD, as she puzzles over the discrepancy between the photos in the cruise brochure and what she sees here. And when small dark children crowd around her legs making peculiar, compulsive opening-and-closing gestures of their tiny hands and tugging on her shorts, repeating, "Money money. Gimme gimme. Money money," and she replies, over and over, "But I don't have any . . ."—forgive her, LORD. Forgive Deena when one frail boy reaches into the side pocket of her cargos, grabs her iPod mini, and tries to run away with it, prompting her to catch him by the arm and yank him right off the ground, the poor kid's so light, he weighs practically nothing. Her iPod falls to the dirt and she stomps her sandal on top of it so none of those other filthy monkeys can steal it, but then the little thief starts crying, piercingly loud, O God, he won't shut up, he won't stop screaming, no matter how much she shakes him . . .

LORD, try to console Deena as she rushes up to her parents in Jimmy Buffett's Margaritaville, where she finds them sitting on stools at a thatched bar with outside air-conditioning and tall, slushy drinks in their hands, and startles them with her tearful outburst—"How long do we have to stay on this stupid island? Can't we just go back to the ship now? Please? Can't we just go back?"

Take a little break now, LORD. You must be tired. Spend a relaxing afternoon at the Cloud 9 Spa. Visit the Limelight Lounge and the Comedy Club; sit with Jerome at the Piano Bar, and try your hand at blackjack in the Lucky Day Casino, before catching up with Deena again a night or two later.

It's Cruise Elegant Evening in the Sapphire Dining Room, an enormous but cool and dim hall on the Mezzanine Deck, and Deena and her parents are being waited on by their regular server, a charming young man from Slovakia named Vladim. He has sharp, dark features and straight dark hair swept back from his forehead. He refills their glasses with wine and water, one gloved hand behind his back, and compliments Deena on her emerald green dress; she blushes and touches her pearl necklace. He tells them about his home country, which none of the Truitts has ever quite heard of before, calling it "the hidden paradise of Europe." For the all-you-can-eat Surf and Turf Special, Bob and Barbara order fruit cocktail, Caesar salad, oysters Rockefeller, and chicken tenders for appetizers; Maine lobster tail, filet mignon, and Italian lasagna for the main course; and baked Alaska, New York cheesecake, and warm chocolate melting cake with vanilla ice cream for dessert (because it's all-you-can-eat, after all). Don't be cross, bountiful LORD, when they forget to thank You for their food; it's only because Bob and Barbara are excited about the lobster, and Deena, You know, hasn't had much of an appetite since her misadventure on Grand Turk a few days ago. She's still thinking about those kids in the slum, wondering why, if You're so great and good, You made those kids so poor and so obviously

70

underfed, while her parents are here slathering their lobster with melted butter, and Bob is dripping pieces of white meat onto his plastic bib, and Barbara is complaining that she can't possibly eat one more bite even as she eagerly saws her filet mignon and lifts another forkful to her mouth . . .

Take a step or two back, LORD, as Deena flings down her own knife and fork and exclaims, "It's disgusting, this much food!" Her parents look up from their plates, baffled. "We're like pigs at a trough!" she says, and, "What did we ever do to deserve this much food? Huh? What?"

"You don't like the lobster?" her father asks, mouth stuffed, but Deena is already up and rushing away from the table, dear LORD, rushing right past You.

Your ways are mysterious and complex, LORD. Sometime later that night, as Deena is wandering by herself through the quiet and empty SportSquare on Deck 12, You lead her right into the path of Vladim, their waiter from dinner. He's leaning against the base of the enormous smokestack and drinking from a small green bottle.

"So you found me," Vladim says, startling Deena.

"Sorry, I wasn't . . ." Deena replies.

"Do not be afraid," Vladim says, stepping out from the shadows. "Do I frighten you? I do not want to frighten you."

He has changed out of his waiter uniform and is wearing distressed blue jeans, a jean jacket with upturned collar, and a white shirt with curious red stitching up and down the front. Here, against the smokestack, without his uniform, he looks smaller, younger and less sure of himself. He smiles quickly at her.

Send a light breeze, O LORD. Let Deena believe that You arranged this encounter, because hasn't she been secretly praying for something exactly like this to happen? Hasn't she seen *Titanic*, and doesn't she know that on a cruise ship, romantic liaisons are practically guaranteed? She wants this, LORD. She needs some affection in her life, and a chance to show that she can be generous and kind in this unfair world. She's still wearing her shiny emerald green dress with the low-cut back and her pearl necklace, and she imagines she must appear quite rich and glamorous to this poor foreign waiter, even though of course she's not, she's just plain old Deena Truitt from Gainesville, and the pearl necklace came from Target and cost practically nothing, for goodness sake. Inspired by the moonlight and the breeze You've sent, she holds onto a support beam of the ropes course and leans away from it, letting her shimmery dress drape out like a fan as she sways to and fro, casual-like. She asks the waiter what he's drinking.

"Would you like some?" Vladim says, and offers her a sip from his bottle of slivovica. He tells her that the drink comes from his hometown, Banská Bystrica, a beautiful city on a river, with mountains and snow skiing and many recreations.

"Pfah!" Deena says, gagging on the liquor. "How can you drink that?"

They talk. Vladim tells her more about Slovakia, the hidden paradise of Europe; Deena pictures castles, dark forests, and dashing young men on horseback. "That sounds awesome," she says, imagining herself there. She tells him about her stupid parents and how she loathes sharing the cabin with them. She manages to drink more of the slivovica. She tells Vladim she's just graduated from high school and is starting college in the fall, at Harvard. A curious expression flashes across his face—he looks like he might burst out laughing—but then he goes on quickly to say that he knew she was older than she looked, maybe 19 or 20, he guessed, which pleases Deena immensely.

Follow them down, O confounding LORD, down to the staff quarters on a low, low deck, one that Deena never even knew existed, a deck that's not shown on any of the ship's maps and is indicated only by an "X" in the service elevator. Vladim leads Deena through a narrow passageway and into his tiny cabin. She eyes the bunk bed built into one wall, and the desk and mirror along the opposite wall. The desk is cluttered with toiletries, a laptop, and a TV tuned to a Spanish-language variety show. Piles of clothes litter the floor, and shirts and pants hang from clotheslines strung against the walls. The cabin smells funky and closed-in; there's barely enough room to turn around. Deena has a feeling that she might be entering into something very foolish, quite possibly dangerous here, but Vladim has already closed and locked the door behind them, and he seems so sincere and needy. Now he's massaging her hand and telling her what a pretty girl she is, what pretty eyes she has, what pretty hair, what a pretty mouth—and, dear LORD, she wants desperately to believe him.

Maybe You'd like to wait outside, LORD. You know what's going to happen anyway. Stroll up and down the passageway; peek in on some of the other cabins while Deena and the waiter do what they must. Because You set them up for this, didn't You, LORD? You answered Deena's naïve prayers. You delivered her right into the arms of this slimy waiter (Vladim? Really, LORD? Could You have created a more obvious villain than this?); and while it's true that Deena went willingly, even eagerly, down to his cabin, do You think she's really ready for this? Barely fifteen years old? How can You stroll up and down with Your hands clasped behind Your back, whistling like that, when You know what's happening right now inside that smelly cabin?

O infuriating LORD. O damnable LORD.

Sneak up on Deena a half hour later high up on the Serenity Deck. There she is, standing at the rail looking out over the bow of the enormous, ugly ship. The Serenity Deck is for adults only, but Deena figured, screw it, what are they going to do, throw her overboard? Behind her, synthesized ocean sounds play from hidden loudspeakers. The wind lifts her dress, swirls around her bare legs.

She didn't like it, LORD, not one bit. Her arms are bruised from where Vladim held her too roughly, and her green dress is ripped along one seam. This is not what it was supposed to be like. This is nothing like the *Titanic*. She feels debased and miserable. And You did this to her, LORD. You did this, didn't You?

The most humiliating part of it all—the one detail she knows she'll remember the rest of her life—was when he refused to let her kiss him. She kept lifting her head to try and plant a kiss on his lips, but he clamped his mouth shut and twisted his face away. Was she really so ugly? Was she so repulsive that he couldn't even tolerate her kiss, even as he grunted and squirmed on top of her? Her dress was bunched up under her chin, his pants on the floor, when she finally shoved him off. She snatched up her shoes and unlocked the door, and still Vladim kept grabbing at her and asking, incredibly, when she would visit him again. He was wearing nothing but his shirt and socks when she fled his cabin, ridiculous long black socks that came up to his knees, that creep.

Gripping the rail, she stares down at the water, at the moonlight silvering the surface, unusually calm tonight. She thinks of those grubby little kids in the slum back on Grand Turk. She thinks of her parents digging into their lobsters. She thinks of all the slights and injustices she's had to endure until now and will undoubtedly have to endure for years to come, and she wonders: What the hell are you up to, LORD? What can You possibly be thinking? Is this some kind of a test? Is that what this is? You mean to teach us, Your children, a lesson? Pardon the profanity, LORD, but what kind of a fucked-up lesson is this?

She stares at the water, gripping the rail so tightly she begins to tremble. She's crying. She's praying to You, LORD. She's begging You. Just one goddamn thing. Just grant her one goddamn little thing she can feel good about. That's all she asks. Or are You really that mean-spirited, LORD? Are You so cruel and low that You'd leave her hanging here at the rail with nothing?

She stares at the water. She stares and stares; she stares so long and hard that she begins to feel sick to her stomach. She wipes her eyes with her arm and is just about to turn around and go back inside—when a low dark wave swells in front of the ship. A strange, craggy hump rolls alongside the hull, and then, unexpectedly, a plume of water sprays into the air, so close she can hear it, like a deep, sad sigh rising up from the bottom of the ocean. A wing-shaped fluke as big as a minivan breaks the surface and flops back down, and then the water closes over it and is still again.

Deena stumbles back from the rail. Holy crap, she thinks. She just saw a whale. She glances left and right to see if anyone else has witnessed this, but the deck is empty, there's no one here but her.

Only she saw it. Only she did.

New Year's Prayer

Until the sound of jean-clad thighs
rubbing together becomes a mating call,
LORD, liberate me

from these rolls. Muffin tops, LORD,
blubber bulging at my waist,
my protective winter layer, let me not be

bat winged, LORD, stretch marks
rising, my body a constellation
of bulge, fat back, LORD, knock knees,

save me from dimpled thigh doom,
these pug faced elbows. When I stop,
LORD, let not my cellulite shake,

aftershocks rumbling in waves
across my ass's awkward smile.

For Target

Dear Arrowhead water, dear feather boa, dear father
and mother with the toddler and cart full of candles:

I wanted to tell you the sky swished open its doors
this morning, the whole shebang slid by on felt,

and I entered the mythic fires of stoicism,
bore my nakedness in the manner of Shackleton,

defiantly ignorant. For I know that Target, centerless
like new pedagogies, loves the good good,

loves punishment somehow instructing
a niche audience. That's me. I love to finger

the Milano-style whatnot, bend the necks
of five-headed floor lamps. Yes, I love you dearly,

dear church of the cherished storage bin,
dear Cheerios and the bowl to drown you in,

dear warehouse sky, dear reindeer aiming the beads
of your eyes at my impulse buys. Once, I shot a gun

in the desert, laid it down in the sand, and said
a small prayer to prayers of small sizes.

Years later, we navigated the marked-downs,
the Doritos safe in Mylar pillows,

thought we'd stripped ourselves clean
of desire's burrs and foxtails, even as popcorn

promised low-sodium transubstantiation.
But we were *registering*, the word itself green, bearded,

so aimed our fantastic machines at the crock
pot and bath rug, at the iPod snug in its skin.

We dressed ourselves in the warmth of that small space
heater, fed the nuisance of class consciousness

little biscuits. How cloudless, how terrible and lucid
the distances we traveled for our dear wedding guests—

dear, which my Italian friend uses in that foreign way,
as in, *That pair of pants is too dear.* And how dear, how sheer

the night, we thought, dearly beloved, outside the Target,
the headlights of all those cars trained on us.

For Those Hung-over On Tuesday

Anoint us, O LORD, and receive our repentance for our journey to the Moran Club last noonday. We humbly repent for the poorly-rolled joint we smoked in the parking lot and lit, by thy providence with our Ford Contour's factory-installed lighter, and for the long drags of local weed we bleweth out our cracked window into the grandeur of thy creation.

In thy mercy, thou relieved us early from our summer labors at the school supply warehouse, and in our depravity, we did not text word of thy mercy to our girlfriend Amy and go to her. Forgive us, Almighty God, for drinking two-dollar drafts for four hours alone before messaging "Moran Club?" to the heaviest drinker on our contact list.

Why, O LORD, did our heart rejoice and did we lavish thy due praise on Pete Kitko, who liveth with his grandmother, when he arrived and bummeth us his cigarettes? Deal graciously with us, Holy God, for the nature in which things escalated. For attempting to go beer-for-beer and then shot-for-shot with Kitko, whose girth is ample. For our leers at our Sister in Christ and bartender, Meghan, whom you made in your perfect image. For having the words to "Bohemian Rhapsody" rote upon our hearts and none of thy holy scripture. For the suggestion we switch from Coors to Makers and from Makers to Wild Turkey. For the second joint, this one very strong and not local at all, smoked in Kitko's Grand Am while REO Speedwagon playeth. For vomiting in the Moran Club men's room sink and not its commode. For the sin of omission in texting "I don't feel good" when dear, sweet Amy wondered if we would come over for dinner.

For leaving our keys hanging out of our front-door lock. For apparently peeing in our hamper.

Shed your grace on Meghan for her wisdom in cutting us off at eight last night. Abide the Contour, O LORD, still parked in the Moran Club lot. Watch over Kitko, who by his girth and steadiness of hand guided us in his Grand Am the mile down Crooked Sewer Road to our door. Steady our stomach and cool our head, Holy Father, while we watch thy Price is Right and drink thy Gatorade. Put around us thy hedgerow of protection from all warehouse managers who were not properly notified of absence by 6 a.m. Grant that Amy might be forever spared from all knowledge which does not behoove her to know. Allow that we might never again be seduced into excesses of neon and black labels.

Fountain of all Wisdom: reveal by your Holy Spirit the thing that must be profoundly wrong with us.

For Vince McMahon and the Tending of the Flock

You, creator of worlds, destroyer of men. You, slick-haired, slick-tongued, the slow rumble of a voice that has been layered with ash and pinecone, the bark of a tree cascading down your throat like it has been there all along—steadfast & rooted in cold ground since before any of us were a thought. We give you praise, we give you thanks, we give you a subtle roar when things go our way: a gentle bow of the head as we appreciate you for you instead of what you have become. You, false god. You, a man full of sweat and sand, you in a suit the color of a beautiful lake, you of a color that you created.

You, one of us: you, the voice, you, in a cheap suit, zipped on, velcroed in the back, you, interchangeable. You, knowing the names of all of the maneuvers as if you invented them: released hold, heel kick, brain buster, back breaker. You, crying after my heroes died. You, steadfast in your presentation. You, presenter of worlds.

Praise to you, hallelujah, praise for every red chested slap, every unification, every beer barrel-chested man I would never become, every long-haired snap back for emphasis, every fake punch meant to look beautiful. Every blonde with space tits, every black man thuggish, every islander from the land of the rising sun. Every dead hero in the mold of a hero, every broken back and every brain busted.

I give myself unto you when my own father does not wish to answer questions; my mother secretly sliding tithes through cable wires to keep her child happy after skinny cruisers lifted his shirt up to expose the hairless fat beneath—the old television of my grandfather's brought home on a Sunday and hooked up by Monday, the first thing I could ever call my own: you amongst

81

drawings of imaginary warriors pulled from magazines—fold out posters where staple holes pierce stomachs that look nothing like mine.

When they ask if I am still loyal, chairman, I am still loyal—I see your fiction in my dreams and wish to be a part of it: to pretend that this is all real and I am here among it; that I am beautiful and beloved, that I am a vampire, that I am from the future, that I am a turkey hatched from an egg. That you have changed my name, rearranged it so it is unrecognizable: that when the crowds chant for me, they spit something new—where too much of my name has been misspelled for too long, that yours is the only true name that is left and it is that of your father. I am still loyal and I praise you with a knowing smile—that I have not changed because you have not changed: that I know all of the tricks—the one about the slap to the thigh, the stomping of the mat, the chair always delivered to the broadest part of the body.

I close my eyes and I am created by you: I am picking brutes over my shoulder, I am spinning them into oblivion. I send them crashing into crumpled heaps, I am hugging the breath out of strangers. I am wrapping my wrists. I am taping my ribs.

And yet there is no room for me here: where there is nothing that creativity can provide other than a quick toss down a flight of stairs. You, god of something I hold dear, break me and make me whole again: make me a businessman with a paisley tie. Make me disappear only to be reborn: a clown for the taking, a golem who eats his own fingers. Put me in a mask that keeps me from breathing.

To God Almighty That I Have Never Believed In, Especially Since This Entity Saw Fit to Take My Best Friend Rosemarie Who Had Just Finished Med School at Johns Hopkins When She Was Killed in a Horrible Car Accident

Oh (H)igher (P)ower in Whom I Have Never Believed, in your vast nothingness please forgive me for every time I have mocked the administrative assistants who work in my office, Carol and Vernita, for their belief in (Y)ou, for all the times I've snorted at their Facebook posts thanking Jesus for another blessing when they get the used Lexus they wanted or their kid survives an ATV accident with nothing more than a broken wrist. What if you, so-called (C)reator of all things [that I don't think actually created anything], do in fact grant administrative assistants' wishes in the form of Alabama football championship wins and money enough to get lapband surgery? If I have been wrong all this time, please don't smite me with your angry fist but rather take pity on me for my failure to believe in you, the Easter Bunny, Santa Claus, The Tooth Fairy, all ghosts, and my chances of ever winning the lottery.

Forgive me, (O)mnipotent (O)ne who I judge to be impotent, for coveting that "Actually, I'm an Atheist" tee-shirt for a $25 contribution to the woman in Moore, Oklahoma who responded to CNN's Wolf Blitzer's query after a tornado ripped through her town, destroying her home, that she must be thanking God for being spared, "actually, I'm an atheist." Forgive me, further, for posting a photo of myself in said tee shirt on Facebook, upsetting Carol and Vernita, the most competent administrative assistants I've ever worked with, who both posted on my wall that my tee shirt makes them sad, and forgive me even further for responding, "Religion makes ME sad." For I have been both sad and righteous in my non-belief since I was but a child, refusing to utter the phrase, "One nation, under

God, indivisible" at the beginning of class at Bayville Elementary School, and believing only and always that the termination of my existence will in fact be an eternal nothingness during which my inert and spiritless body will be followed on by my slow decomposition until my body finds its ultimate form as garden mulch or fine ash.

And when I wept uncontrollably at my best friend Rosemarie's wake after she died in her Volkswagen Jetta that jumped the divider while she reached for a hairbrush, and hit a semi-truck that killed her instantly, forgive me for my response when the priest came up to me and said I should not be sad because Rosemarie now had eternal life. For I sneered at him and continued my weeping unabated. I wept because Rosemarie was my best friend and because she had so patiently tutored me in her parents' roach-infested kitchen so that I could bring up my math SAT scores above 500 (I ended up with a 520) and because she had just finished medical school at Johns Hopkins and furthermore because for the first time in her life had met a nice guy named Steve who was planning to marry her which would mean she'd have sex for the first time, because Rosemarie was a good Catholic who went to mass every Sunday and genuflected when she drove past St. Gertrude's, the Catholic Church in our town where I would years later deliver her eulogy and then go take a piss in the basement bathroom with my Mom and joke with her at least we'd gotten to piss in a church.

O (N)onexistent (A)lmighty, explain to me why the one person you'd allow to die among all my friends and acquaintances, hundreds of ne'er do wells and layabouts, would be Rosemarie Reid, who went to medical school on a ROTC scholarship and consequently had to spend weekends learning how to shoot a gun, who was never a good driver, who drove her mother's Chevy Caprice into one of the stone pillars flanking her street right after she got her driver's license. Who sat on two phone books to drive because she was too short to see over the steering wheel, and who would bring to mind, upon hearing of her death, Alan Turing, the computer genius who chose not to drive a car but instead to ride his bicycle to work every day because his mind was too occupied with higher concepts for him to focus on driving a car? O, I am pained when I think of the moment when my sister called me on the phone to tell me Rosemarie had died and I collapsed on the floor and bruised my coccyx. And then later that day, O (I)maginary (D)eity, when I called my friend Pam to tell her the bad news, how she said, "Well, Ro was never a very good driver," and though nearly apoplectic with rage and sadness at the cruelty of the universe I laughed anyway, because what Pam said was not just funny but also true. Because truth and laughter are all we have in this world to believe in.

For Lubbock

LORD, protect we freaks through the haboobs and the heat, through hailstorms and wild hogs and three-legged dogs licking themselves raw in filthy dirt alleys; we, of the no good places to eat, we of the town run by cattle and cotton, where daily the parks fill up with trash that is taken by wind into yards of cracked dirt and weeds and extended cab, overtall, chrome-hubcapped pickups; protect me, LORD, somehow, from my fellow West Texans—those You've left to rot here, on these Staked Plains, among pig farms and wheat fields and cartel drop houses; take the holes from our streets and the guns from our holsters and give us bike lanes, Oh LORD, and let us glimpse hybrids, and let our town, somehow, Dear, Mighty LORD, embrace the concept of curbside recycling, so our teenagers, having swilled all their Boone's, and well on their way to getting each other pregnant, might not add their bottles to gutters already clogged with glass, but never with condoms, for Jesus is contraception here, LORD, and it seems our teens' prayers often go unanswered; but I thank you, too, LORD, for this glimpse of Hell, for showing me a place so shitty and crooked and mean that I now understand just how bad it can be: the tap water wrecked, the sky raining mud, evolution laughed at, your bullshit much better.

For Those Haunted by Deceased Parents, Lost Youth, Missed Connections, Misspent Friendships, Spent Looks, Dropped Balls, Roads Not Taken, Words Not Spoken, Words Spoken, Dampened Passions, Failures of Both Business and Imagination, Bad Calls, Mixed Bags, Sagging Flesh, Spilt Milk, Bad Blood, and Random Acts of Unkindness

Make of our hollowed hearts a bowl.
Receive us. Forgive us.
Fill us, pour into us awe.

For Men Named Nancy

Everliving LORD who is not named Nancy as we are, grant us the strength to not read too much into that look someone just gave us as they asked, "Isn't Nancy a girl's name?" Protect us from over-reacting when someone brings up that Jonny Cash song about a boy named Sue—Yes, we have heard it and yes it is relevant, but we have grown weary of having the same conversation over and over, sweet LORD, Amen.

For Heated Swimming Pools

Dear God, we thank thee for heated swimming pools. In this day and age, when water is extra-precious, and climate change is upon us, and the weather is fierce and strange, heated swimming pools shimmer quietly in the manicured lawns of east coast mansions, in the concrete and treeless interior courtyards of midwestern motels, astride the rocky cliffs of prefab beach retreats in southern California, and in their prevalence, in our great nation, they speak of your generosity.

Dear LORD, you made the ocean in its unfathomable hosting of life, you made the womb in its unfathomable hosting of life, and you also made heated swimming pools, which are neither unfathomable, nor, hopefully, hosting too much life. They are, among other things, a way for us to experience warm water—gallons upon gallons of warm water—and although they can be deadly, and many towns pass laws where they must be fenced in so that small, un-swimming children do not fall in them, they also serve as a playground of unparalleled delight.

Dear God, thank you for all holes which are meant for delight, all wet and possibly not- completely-clean holes. Thank you for the greatest and most under-appreciated quality of holes, which is their receptivity. Let us pause a moment now, to observe how we treat the astonishing receptivity of a heated swimming pool, to notice how we cram it with a riot of horrific plastic pool toys, how we infuse it with chemicals to keep it free of creatures and finally, how we belly flop into it, with our own sweaty and slickly sunscreened bodies.

Dear God, we recognize our stupidity in all things regarding our environment, and we pray that we may we become smarter, and, in doing so, may we model the wisdom of a heated swimming pool. May we receive your love and your intelligence like a heated swimming pool. May we receive our new neighbors, the spilled lemonade, skinny dipping, and all joy and calamity with the same reflective wisdom that is the heated pool—steadfast, honest, warm, responding in exact degree to the force and motion exerted upon us, cannonball after scream-y cannonball.

May we receive your fountain of love, the one we keep hearing about but which we haven't actually experienced personally, as naturally and unfazed-ly as the heated swimming pool receives the pee of small children, laughing ecstatically in their water wings.

And LORD, when the time comes, when the dire prediction of climate change more fully manifests and the people of our great nation have contracted together and headed north as a migrating herd, when the concept of a single family's heated swimming pool will seem as outrageous to us as, say, bloodletting and trepanning do now, may there be some compassion for the people we were, that is, the people we are, the people who jumped in, and swam, and maintained these pools, who fussed and argued over their temperature, and may there be grace for the pool maintenance men who scurried about them, holding the long handles of the skimming nets, and for the children who learned to swim in them, and for the precious fuel we used to warm them, for lo, in the end, the heated pool reflects our desire to return to the womb, to the place where we were formed, where it was warm and wet, and all was possible.

And for that wish, may we be forgiven. Amen.

For Saturday Mail

God of Deliverance, we thank you for the many years you saw fit to bless us with Saturday mail:

A rich tradition dating back to the apostles' epistles.

Would those church-bound bundles have made it to their bickering awaiters if not for Saturday mail? We're not sure. We're hazy on how it worked then.

But we know how it works now, and how it doesn't. We know the feelings we feel when our mails fail.

How our boxes are flooded, carelessly, with letters for neighbors and none for us.

If we had to give the feeling a name, LORD, it'd be called: I Thought This Was America.

For so long, the work of our Postal Service mimicked your own works: 6 days of activity and then a much-deserved rest.

But the Postal Service has turned away from your ordinances.

They've scorned you in their hearts and danced round the gilded altar of the pagan LORD of Cutbacks.

We feel like breaking stone tablets over our knees sometimes. We understand the impulse.

Obviously the rise of UPS and FedEx couldn't have helped.

Obviously the internet (and email specifically) had a role.

Obviously postage is pricy.

Obviously when someone my age writes a real physical letter to someone my age, it is so they can gush about the experience on-line, implying a schedule chock full of life-well-lived indicators.

But then we once heard on NPR that the Postal Service's money woes are almost entirely wrapped up in this law where the USPS must have cash on hand for the future pensions of all current employees, which is not the expectation for any other public institution. That seems fucked.

We admit, LORD, that as with so many things, we did not fully appreciate Saturday mail until it was gone.

We were given to say, "How come the Saturday mail always sucks?"

and "The Saturday guy looks like a creeper—why can't our regular lady come on Saturdays too?"

and "Why didn't they take my outgoing mail? Even though I didn't have any incoming mail, they should have checked. I deserve for them to have checked."

We're sorry, God. We're sorry, gods. We're sorry, Saturn.

We're sorry, Sun and Moon and Mars and Mercury and Thor.

But also we're not sorry and things ought to be better.

This is our main plea for now and we're pretty fired up about it.

When you've sorted this mail issue, we can move on to other petitions.

Next up? Drone strikes, surely—all those poor children. Or else all our delays at the DMV.

For Hypochondriacs

For those who examine every sniffle, for those who chew their lips raw at every mole and freckle, for those with convenient allergies, who feel vertigo before cleaning the house, who mask body hate under lactose intolerance, we pray. And for those who are truly sick, but theatrically.

LORD, forgive those who contract the flu from their flu shots and those who have uprooted their families in pursuit of a dander-free state. For though they are deceitful, they are only deceiving themselves and they suffer greatly enough for this sin.

And for their doctors, LORD, who must explain hysterical pregnancy, who must prescribe aspirin, who must prescribe a trip to the bathroom, send Your blessing. Look down on those who have removed gall bladders when all tests turned up empty, for they would otherwise be called quacks, otherwise lose their patients to countless second opinions, for they must remember the times they got it wrong, a dismissed nothing turned to Celiac. Grant them guidance, oh LORD, and confidence in their diagnoses.

LORD God, who sent Your only Son to heal us all; He who made the blind see and the lame walk; who took His vacation with lepers and spent His working hours with tax collectors and women; who surely have their own diseases. Bless us with a patience only one who was crucified can understand. Grant us patience with our roommates and napping family members, those who cannot come dancing because their bodies are swelling. Though the answer to "how are you?" is always too honest, help us to continue asking. Help us learn when to nod and when to say, "that's awful" instead of catching them in a lie.

For we too have experienced illness, a mother shut away with cancer, sickness the only real way to know her. For we too had scoliosis surgery as children, and the back brace, though cause for teasing, was our first taste of attention, our first understanding of what it is to be special. Our greatest fear, though we try to trust in Your salvation, is our mortality, and we too feel it in our every stumble and cough. LORD, you sent Your only Son to heal us from the sickness of sin, however imaginary, and in Your holy name, we pray.

For Everyday Punks

As we walk through the shadows in the alleys, we wear this button, this vestment, this testament to Dinosaur Jr. with the courage of our convictions. We wait for beer in crowded bars, stand in line at the post office, push shopping carts through Target on Sunday afternoons, visit our grandmothers in nursing homes with this little pin that an ex-girlfriend made us fastened tightly above our breast. Like a priest's starched collar. Our 1-inch middle finger to the federal culture.

Though we haven't seen Julie in 15 years, we carry this relic in memory of trading Christmas gifts on her apartment floor the night the semester ended. We honor the walk afterwards to a show in a basement across town. We praise the snow banks, the winter air, the view from the center of the street. We remember an innocence. A time we were proud to identify with feedback and drive – tones we believed in. LORD, we hold vigil. We give thanks. And we ask that you strengthen our spirit.

God, let our faith sound like breaking glass. Steady and guide our hurt and bruised actions as we walk through the lion's den. Inspire and transform our disdain. Despite the raw and punishing world; despite suburbs and strip malls, expensive suits and conference calls, Rush Limbaugh; despite oil spills, IEDs, the price of gasoline, "love" but not for LGBTs; despite all the rude grocery shoppers and drunk drivers and behind-the-wheel-texters, politicians, bosses, cops and drug charges; despite Wall Street, Walmart and assault rifles, high school reunions, dick pics, the minimum wage, those running shoes with toes; despite *American Idol* and MTV and every FM host replaced by a computer; despite Michelob Ultra, any bar that charges more than a dollar for Pabst; despite punishing hangovers, waking up with sore knees, heavy handled stomachs, athlete's foot, male pattern baldness, blood pressures, cancer; despite losing those we love; despite wakes, funerals, burials; despite the hollow space when the heart implodes; despite returning to campus after winter break and learning Julie had slept with a ski instructor in Colorado; despite all things great and small, you remind us of the joy left on earth. That tender moment - like after taking a punch to the face - when we realize we spin amidst something bigger and far more reaching. Something fucking huge.

We find new melodies in the distortion. Once dead, now resurrected noisy, charged, and sweet. Healer of wounds, you sucked the venom from J., Lou, and Murph. You exhaled into the corpse and enabled us to love a band again. Though Dinosaur Jr. may have lost their youth, they have not lost vision and in this we are empowered. In this you redeem us from death, heartache, and shitty music. We trust in your fuzzed-out, jangled-pop plan, God.

And we understand our calling. Should an enemy - one who opposes ideas like individuality, expression, authenticity, and general rowdy fun - beat us down, we will not remain fallen. We will rise again with shield and sword raised. With this little button we walk the path of the righteous and take pride in spreading your word to the heathens. *It's a Dinosaur Jr. album called* Bug. *Yeah, you should check it out.* We march forward. We start choppin'. Amen.

For Mothers Who Dread the Dentist

O MERCIFUL GOD, and heavenly Guardian of the ADA, who hast taught us in thy holy Word to not only brush twice a day with a soft-bristled brush, but that thou dost not willingly afflict infections in the upper left bicuspid of mothers under 55 without dental insurance. Look with pity, no floss, we beseech thee, upon the hunger for solid food of thy servant for whom our prayers are offered. Extract the suffering and all her top teeth but the incisors. Remember her, O LORD, in mercy for all her molars no longer there; endue her soul with patience and partial dentures: comfort her with a sense of thy goodness and a thick cut rib-eye medium-rare: lift up thy countenance upon her imminent closed lip smile, and give her teeth for her only daughter's upcoming wedding; through Crest and Colgate our ADA. *Amen.*

For My Daughter, Who Does Not Exist

Bless you, my hollow child, lying under nothing tonight
in one of those other worlds. Let there be wind, for there is
no wind. Let me hear it and fear nothing for you.

Bless your yawning, unreal mouth, your even breath.
When you wake, will your first word be *Daddy*
or *God?* Let it be *God*, let there be that.

Bless your fingers playing on my face, in my hair,
under my skull. Let there be your soft touch, for there is
no touch. And let there be the light crescent moons of your nails.

Bless everything you will do and all your dreams.
Dream of your father. Dream of your god. Let there be
years and years and years, for there is no future.

And since between each world there is nothing,
let there be a prayer. Let me bless your too-pale skin,
your too-auburn hair, your beautiful impossibility.

For the Preteen Girl

Our Father who art in Heaven, please protect this preteen in all her glorious early pubescence. Show her the way of her love, the truth of her beauty, and the light of her intellect. May you cradle her oily, pimpled, ruddy face in your eternally accepting hands and say unto her that the Todds and the Brads do not define her worth. Nay, nor the Seths, nor the Jonathans, nor the Seans, neither when they forget her name despite its having been encapsulated with theirs inside dozens of penciled hearts in her notebook, neither when they snap her training bra strap on the way to health class, neither when they tell her to move her lard-ass on the bus, LORD. For verily, they do not define her worth. Nay, even when they push her against the rough stucco wall behind the gym, Oh LORD, to introduce their young spearmint tongues into her mouth, neither in this splendorous moment of deliverance wherein she believes she is now among the chosen ones shall they ascribe her value, though she will not understand so at the time. For the uninitiated know not the ways of the world. Watch over her, Father, when she sees another girl shrieking with overly boisterous laughter as she gets a piggy back ride from that very same Todd or Brad or Seth at the fall carnival a few days later. Protect her when that boy, whose agitated fingers had fumbled against the rise of her budding chest not 72 hours prior says unto her, with eyes averted, "Oh, yeah, hey, what's up," as she approaches him trembling with nerves, and she feels the scrutiny of his friends and sees the contempt upon the faces of those other girls, the newly chosen, with their hands on their hips, legs angled forward, heads tilted behind curtains of hair, blackness and insecurity in their own hearts. "Do you know this fugly bitch?" they will ask the Todd or the Brad or the Seth and he will shrug and the girls will titter while they all walk away in a cluster of scorn, for mankind knows no greater capacity for cruelty than the preteen girl toward another preteen girl. Father, unbind her nerves when that moment freezes her feet in place and flushes her face. Cast out the devil of self loathing that will rise within her. Release her from the ever inward-turning disdain spreading through her body like toxic mold creeping in the dark hollows of damp walls.

Father, we pray you may choose to make this preteen bleed for the first time at a far more opportune moment than 11 a.m. on a Tuesday, as she sits in pale peach shorts in Biology class, so that when she rises, she will leave not the scandalous red mark of her newly arrived womanhood upon the seat beneath her for her peers to see. Spare her, Heavenly Father, from walking through the hallway with the scarlet bloom of thy gift emblazoned upon her backside, on display for the Todds and Brads and Seths, for the Kristens and Siennas and Megans. Spare her, Heavenly Father, from acquiring the nickname "Bulls-eye" into perpetuity. *For the love of you*, oh Father, we beseech you, let her become aware *before* she reaches Math class, where her best friend will whisper the unseemly verity to her just as the bell rings and Mr. Levine tells everyone to sit down and take out their pencils for a test. Still her rasping sobs, Father, from inside the stall of the girls' bathroom when she sees the evidence for herself. By thy grace, provide for her a blessed sweatshirt, LORD, to tie around her waist as she walks to the nurse's office. Calm the anxiety over her body's betrayal, the abrupt loss of her physical childhood, the embarrassing confession to her parents and her mother's shopping basket filled with mortifying maxi pads and tampons. Almighty God, please, we beg of you, be merciful. Just allow this girl to get her first period at 8 PM at home. Ferry her gently from child to adult. Shield this preteen girl, Oh LORD, for verily, thy world shall be difficult enough as she claws her way awkwardly from girl to woman and learns her place in the world. Let her go forth in peace, we beseech you.

In the name of the Holy Spirit. Amen.

For Those Loitering In Front of Quik Chek, Madera, Pennsylvania, July 1998

For the children of fathers who work wiring blasting caps in the strip mines, the kids in JNCO jeans and Tool T-shirts who steal their mothers' long cigarettes and clip the filters with pocket knives so they pull like regulars. For the adolescents who drink warm Genesee out of emptied ice-tea cartons and carve their names in the white paint of the newspaper machine. For the shirtless boys riding in circles in the potholed parking lot on bikes with bent back rims and salvaged frames. For the ones who live on the hill by the closed clothing factory and sit on the Quik Chek's curb waiting for Dilbert to come out of the fire hall and buy them snuff. For the younger brothers who are shot with pellet guns and hung upside-down from telephone poles until they sob for help. For the younger sisters who spray their bangs with dollar-cans of White Rain and have hardened their speech. And for their older brothers sitting on the loading dock by the shit crick who have never seen the ocean or been on a plane, who skip school and watch the loaded tri-axles trail coal dust. For everyone out in front of Quik Chek who has already learned the thing they are best at is not giving a fuck. Let them burn with this certainty and grant it sufficiency. In your grace, give them jobs in the gas fields, and in their exhausted sleep, visions of the sublime. Suffuse their drives to work in the dark mornings with that peace beyond understanding. May the air from the plastic vents blow hot on their hands. Keep the deer watchful and still on the embankments.

Circus Prayer

Dear LORD,

Thank You for letting me survive the seedy and derelict circus that showed up on the ball fields of my New Jersey elementary school in 1979. If You recall, there were two shows: the early and the late, and I went to the former. I remember the pair of tigers sitting on pedestals with metal collars, the O-rings at the ends of their heavy chains affixed to steel spikes driven into the outfield. There was no fence or wall between the tigers and the incoming circus-goers. There was no cage of any sort. No, Dear LORD, the only dividers were landscaping timbers resting horizontally on cinderblocks, not more than a foot off the ground. A single line of those timbers created the only "barrier" as the patrons streamed into the tent. But anyone, from an adult to a toddler, could have easily stepped over and walked right up to a tiger if they had had the *cajones*. Could have easily, if so inclined, slapped one of the beasts across its beautiful whiskered face.

It was at the late show where all the excitement happened. But I wasn't at that show, Dear LORD. No, for whatever reason, You found it in my best interest to go to the early one. And I remember that after the incident, as a nine year old, I was angry with You. Not because You let the tragedy happen. No, instead I was angry (and also jealous) because I wasn't there to witness it while many of my friends were. You chose to have me at home as that tiger leapt off its pedestal with just enough play in its chain to pounce on the boy, a boy my age from the next town over, who had strayed to the wrong side of that useless little barrier. Who had his neck bitten, mauled, and eaten by a three hundred? four hundred? five hundred? pound tiger. Who was killed by that tiger in front of a tent-full of onlookers. Who was pulled from the jaws of the beast by our school's custodian, Mr. Van Sulkama, albeit, a tad too late.

The following day, Dear LORD, the circus had fled. But at recess I, along with a girl from my class, found a bloody, goopy pile of something in the grass near third base. Something the size and color of a juvenile eggplant. A deep purple that resembled smashed poke berries. Thirty years later, after I located the girl on Facebook, I asked if she remembered that goopy pile or was it something my young mind had invented. She remembered.

And the parents LORD, oh, the parents. Two sets in this instance. Because You didn't have the boy go with his own parents, no, but with the parents of a friend. So *they* were responsible for the boy's wellbeing. How does one live with that sort of guilt for the rest of their lives? And then the actual parents, LORD. They send their son off to the circus and he never comes back? Not abducted or kidnapped, not killed in a car accident, but eaten by a tiger? How many parents, in the history of all parents in civilization, can say their child was killed in such a way? A hundred maybe? Ever? And at least if it was in India or wherever tigers still roam, at least then the parents could make some sort of sense of it. Still painful, yes, but it could be rationalized. But in New Jersey, LORD? How do the parents begin to make heads or tails of that one? How awkward must that conversation be, even thirty years later, when new acquaintances ask innocent questions about family, maybe while at a dinner party and they see an old photo of the boy on the wall? "Oh, who is that handsome little guy?" And then the mother, or maybe the father, tries to explain. Why would You do that to those poor parents? Were they atheists or something? Had they denounced Your name at some point way back when?

Is it bad, Dear LORD, that I wanted to be there that night? To see that boy ripped open and partially eaten by a tiger? Why did You spare me that, yet, in Your infinite wisdom, allow me outside for recess the very next day to find the boy's viscera lying in the hot sunshine beneath a swarm of hungry green-bottle flies? To let my imagination run wild with disturbing visions possibly more horrific than if I'd just witnessed the actual event? I know I'm not supposed to question the whys of Your ways, Dear LORD, but I'm asking anyway because quite frankly, it doesn't make a whole lot of damn sense. No sense that I can see anyway. As You well know, I'm not much on praying, so I'm not sure about etiquette here. How does the prayer stop? Do I thank you? Do I cross myself or leave some offering? Or do I just end it, and hope that somehow You'll reply?

For the Moth, But Also for the Spider

O SOMEONE come save this moth outside our window, flapping for two hours and longer. Its spread wings are the size of an outstretched hand, its body as solid as a man's thick thumb.

For hours we have been watching it, our own hands tight in our laps. We did not even notice the spider web stretched outside our front window until the moth was trapped inside it. Wings beat like a bird's against the glass, and we think surely, no web can hold this. But hours pass and the moth still fights to free itself, we still sit in the living room, watching it fail from the comfort of our couch.

We root for the moth, and if it can hear us, it must think, *what assholes*. To remain spectators, to not rise and help. But we have learned somewhere that moths are fragile, that their wings will brush apart in our hands, that we should let nature take its course.

LORD, there is also the spider to consider. A fraction of the moth's size, it spins as quickly as the wings thrash, trying to swaddle the moth into death. The spider darts closer, rapt and needy, leaps back when the moth announces itself again: No, not yet, I am not finished. The wings are windfall and wind, possibility of feast or of disaster. The spider is so exhausted, it will need to eat. And if the moth escapes, and leaves the web in ruins? We cheer for the moth, LORD, and beseech you to aid it. But then we think of the spider.

And then we think of ourselves, sitting in our living room, cheering. The television is off, cell phones set aside. How pure this is, this kind of entertainment. One might almost think we were the kind of people who knew the names of trees, who could identify this breed of moth, this species of spider. Who would not watch this like a nature documentary or a thriller, Moth/ra vs. Spider. Who would not pat themselves on the back for not growing bored, not calling up an Internet video of the exact same thing happening to some other moth, some other spider. We stay focused, at least, on the creatures at hand.

Years later I look them up; I scan through pictures, Latin names, looking for a set of enormous, white, flailing wings. *Antheraea polyphemus*, perhaps, a nocturnal moth drawn to brightness. It was all our fault, the porchlamp we kept so casually lit—not for safety, just to welcome ourselves home. We were spendthrifts of light, and a clever spider made its web inside our vanity. We lured this moth to its suffering. We needed it to escape so we were escaped from blame.

Does this offend you, LORD? Is this one more thing for which we must ask your forgiveness? And will it be forthcoming, if you had no mercy for the moth, nor the spider, nor someday for us, O invisible, almighty, and eternal God?

Because that moth is years dead now, whatever happened in the hours after we finally went to sleep. The spider also, gone to dust. And we, who emerged that next morning to find the moth gone but also the spider, the web a ragged remnant moving in the breeze the screen door made on its hinges: we are all still among the living. All of these your mysteries and your works, O LORD, the answerless empty web and the years since and the sunshine in which we left the house that morning. We left in sunshine, we returned in sunshine, to the sturdy house and the screen door that made a breeze that moved the web. Let us live in such a house all the days of our lives.

And please, LORD, let not those days, nor the strength of our house, depend on our worthiness to inhabit them. Let the wings that beat the window be only your angels, and let them not find us wanting. Grant grace to the moth, but also to the spider, and also to the watchers, their faces peeking from the windows of their sturdy house.

For a Friend Who Has Deactivated Her Facebook Account

O GOD, whose merciful wisdom reaches to the uttermost parts of creation, including social media, please watch over and guide our friend Haley who as of last night or very early this morning deactivated her Facebook account and none of us know why. Assist us, O LORD, as we seek to understand the reason for Haley's vanishment from our news feeds, and strengthen us so that we might bear the burden of grief, worry, and confusion her absence inflicts upon us, even though we haven't actually seen or spoken to Haley since our senior year in high school during which she always had a smile on her face (though who knows what she was smoking in the parking lot every morning, our own recollections of those mornings being somewhat vague). Perhaps Haley's cheerfulness was a brave front even then, Lord, to cover up deep-seated psychological problems which might explain why now she would just suddenly and rudely abandon her eight hundred Facebook friends with no explanation whatsoever. Please help us to support and comfort Haley, O heavenly father, if she deactivated her Facebook account because she's suffering from a life-threatening illness or injury from a car wreck that was totally not her fault (like what happened to us last year with that school bus), or if she's in the midst of a break-up with her fiancé Chad whom we have never met personally but who looks like a nice guy – except for his weird plump lips which appear to be cosmetically enhanced – in Haley's thousands of Facebook photos which as of this morning we can no longer see, photos she may have posted, we now imagine, because the relationship was already toast and she was trying to put a good face on things. And if by chance Haley recently learned that Chad is gay, which frankly we suspected all along based on his obviously injected lips (and also he reminds us of a guy we dated for an entire semester in college who suddenly turned gay for no reason) we ask that you please sustain Haley with your grace and steadfast reassurances, for example that gay men only date the most beautiful women, which we know is true because our ex-boyfriend told us this himself when he suddenly turned gay and dumped us after an entire semester of pretending to be perfectly happy with us. O LORD, we wonder whether Haley's cat Potemkin died, would that be enough of a tragedy to make her deactivate her Facebook account (and what kind of pretentious name is Potemkin, but then Haley always was a poseur, now that we think about it, carrying around that copy of *Being And Nothingness* even though it wasn't required for any class), or maybe she is being cyber-stalked by someone, such as an ex-boyfriend (probably not Chad, LOL, and anyway they were still "in a relationship" as of last night), could that be the reason for her disappearance, or does she just suddenly think she's too good for Facebook, and, by extension, us?

O LORD, please let us know if Haley is mad at us.

Seriously, God. Is Haley is mad at us?

If Haley is mad at us, O blessed God, please enlighten us as to *why*, since we have never failed to like her status updates even though we ourselves are not vegan nor do we have any interest in eating local, going green, thrifting, upcycling, repurposing, Etsy, Andy Borowitz, relief efforts in Rwanda, or any other of Haley's ridiculous liberal hobbies. Nevertheless we frequently and generously comment on Haley's posts that we are praying for her and that it's never too late to accept Jesus as her Lord and Saviour, and if she would just make straight her path, she would obtain everlasting life, like we did. So please look with favor upon us, almighty Father, since obviously if Haley is mad at us she is wrong and deserves your loving correction and swift punishment for the poor choices she has made, especially the choice to deactivate her Facebook account as if our feelings don't mean anything to her, as if our very existence doesn't even matter.

For the Shy, Sad Children of Divorce Who Never Wanted to Go Fishing in the First Place

Cut the line, LORD. Cut it with your big, invisible God shears before all the sad children of divorce, whose uncles have gone back to their cars for fresh packs of cigarettes, begin to reel and heave and reel and heave, as they've been shown, all the while imploring the universe to allow enough line to last until those uncles return so they won't have to wrangle the fishes themselves with trembling hands. So we pray: LORD, cut the line.

Cut it before those children who fear attention even more than they fear the lack of it feel the eyes of the other grown-ups—the strangers, the Lake Michigan fishermen standing like sentries at the water's edge, looking out over the placid infinity, Styrofoam Dunkin' Donuts cups of coffee steaming in their hands, their poles angled on rests—settling upon them, watching them, pulling at their anxiety as the moon pulls up the tides. So we pray: LORD, cut the line.

Cut it before the willowy, indoorsy children, spot their fishes breaking the surface of the lake and feel the sweat slicking the surface of their skin despite the cold morning air, and must lift the beasts into the air and lower the butt of their poles to the sand so that, because they have not yet hit their promised growth spurts, they are nearly eye-to-eye with the flopping, swinging fishes of who-the-hell-knows-what-species. So we pray: LORD, cut the line.

Cut it before the children feel a momentary sense of confidence as they remember how their uncles eased hooks from cheeks and set their own catches in coolers half-filled with lake water, only to slowly understand that their fishes have taken the hooks whole, swallowed them down, tiny whales ingesting even tinier worm Jonahs, and—still aware of the eyes of those around them—are overtaken by terror as they know they must act, but how, how? So we pray: LORD, cut the line.

Cut it before, confused and embarrassed but certain that this is all in some inscrutable way their own fault (*Everything I touch*, they think, *Everything I touch...*), the children take that line in their hands, winding it around their index fingers, and tug, finding a soft but insistent resistance, their hearts hammering in their birdish chests, and then tug again, feeling such shame, such sorrow, and again as their fishes' insides begin to crack free of their bindings, and the fishes jump in their hands in final attempts to escape the torture (are you watching, LORD?), and then they finally pull the pitiful things' guts from their mouths, red and gray masses of organs and membrane now hanging from the hooks. So we pray: LORD, cut the line.

Cut it so that this memory does not linger well into their own adulthoods, appearing in their minds each time they set sight on that gorgeous lake, polluting their conception of it, trans-forming it into a great, soggy madeleine, reminding them not only of those poor fishes so cruelly disemboweled, but of all that came in the months prior to these mornings on the sandy waterfront, of how they came to be there, of their mothers and fathers asunder. So we pray: LORD, cut the line.

Cut it so that, instead of all this, these children, if they have to be here on this shoreline in the frigid cold for their own good (they have been told so many times), might continue to watch the sun come up over the far edge of the lake, their eyelids languorous, their minds only half-present as they take in the rare and celebrated sight, and say to their uncles as they return from their cars, *Nope, no bites* (*Think again*, say the uncles, point-ing fresh, smoldering Parliaments at the slack threads drooping from the ends of the poles), and then wonder unbothered what kind of fishes they might have been that got away and where in this vast body they are now. So we pray: LORD, cut the line.

For the Middle School Boy and His Intemperate Prurience

O GOD ALMIGHTY, whose omnipotent gawk illuminates gloom and penetrates the most viscous grimes, bless the addled essence of the middle school lad, for endlessly and lustfully beleaguered is he. His attention unspanned. His glands at maximum throb. His skin abandoned to excrescence, and all this even while his unruly shins unduly splint. Also do we beseech Thee, burden him not with prolific dandruff. Nor greater gaps of overbite. Nor more inordinance of shoe-size, as his already is—relative to such hairless pegs and enwarted knees—that of a gouted and vagrant clown.

All this we pray, and even as, in Your mercy, we beg of You to stem the relentless stoicism of his feral crotch. Please do so, Father, with fitting visions of fiery lakes and Antichrist minions, of castrator claws and maws. While further we entreat Thee, in accordance with Your vast grace, do please quickly quell his burgeoning body fetor, its hints of saddest molasses and unattended litter box, how these egregious notes uncoil incessantly from his gangly form—O, which reminds us...

Forget not, All-Knowing One, to either erase or increase—really, Your divine choice—that paucity of mustache. Neither quite hair nor fur, it is blight to both lip and passing eye. And speaking of must and ache, let him not, or never again, amidst assembly nor reunion, bring the hidden to unzipped light. Amen? And hitherto, fill not his dreams, O God, with anime gam, nor fang-bitten lip, nor cleavage that overfloweth its cups. Halleluiah, Father, and as Your wisdom abides, do nix finally his ungainly urges for glazing that unwieldy selfhood with topical rubefacient heat rubs? Or, worse, his drive to congress with manners of mechanical suction? Likewise, Almighty, let his game-controller calluses not finger-linger nor wander immorally over the babysister's brassieres or the sisters' glossiest *Cosmo*. For that matter, keep him at bay from the prettiest class-mate's tampon stash, so much feminine care pilfered from her purse only be sniffed furtively, then puffed parodically—mysteri-ous ways!—as a cigar, a cigarette, a cigarillo.

Meaning, Greatest God of All, so too seal off his lungs from ba-nana smoke, his lips from nutmeg, and his testes from tumors that take wing with red bulge, oozing lime green and monstrous from a taurinated bloodstream (which, by the way, must also be shielded from diabetes in, say, the manner his anabolic avatars are shielded from the slings and arrows of hyper-Botoxed valk-eries).

Additionally, O Heavenly One enthroned in pure light, grant the boy relief beyond understanding. Lead him not into qualms of hirsute palms, deformed engorgement, or insufficient girth. Rather, protect him from dreams of lost locker combos, as You protect him daily from expired sack lunches (festering their warm blue fleece) and myriad mishaps of retainer (damn gluey gadget and its mighty dislodges of saliva, causing classmates to gag and tile-slip, begging bully hoards to lick and smear his sad-dest of Grandpa glasses, thus blinding him even as that timid colon aches to burst from spoiled holding)—

O, but it shall not burst! For just as You stilled the Sea of Gali-lee, Thou shalt, Creator of cloud and firmament, provide for him serenity and courage to move his bowels within even the most door-less of public stalls. The same serenity and courage You grant his mother in touching the fabrics he's inurned deep in the hamper, as if she doesn't know, as if she doesn't wish he'd disappear into those radio-crooned ballads that are, right now, filling him with nebulous want, like a puppy that loves without ceasing, that spazzes without fainting, or doe, gut-shot, panting for water, yearning, yearning, infinitely yearning for Heavenly gates alone...

For the Battering of Heart in the Matter of Our Daughter, That She May Rise and Stand, O'erthrown by Thee and Made New

Dear LORD, we ask that our little girl learn the lines that her mama and me have taught her. Lines that you yourself done spewed on Joseph of Nazareth and on all those who would listen thereafter. Lines that our little girl must memorize to recite for when they put her up in the box. Truth is, we all know it's true, her mama and me. *The spirit comes when it will, upon those ferocious wings.* Says she does too, our little girl. Says she knows it's true. Never one to argue, she. Dutiful little servant. And it's best to believe. Best for us all. Such faith she puts in us, her parents. Such a child of faith and faithful ways, our little girl. Please help her to learn those words, LORD. *She was visited upon.* And that's the fulsome truth, LORD. Yea, that you help her to memorize and speak that truth. We ask this in Your Name. And You know we did our part. Before they took us. Taught her those words, LORD, said them along with her, again and again, in her little room, watched her small lips purse and pucker, her eyes frightful in their concentration: *Visited upon, Visited Upon, Visited Upon.* And we put her in her pretty plaid Sunday school dress, in her little pink bedroom, on her bed, reading the Bible. We did this immediately after the school called, when they said they were concerned, when they said she was bleeding on her school seat, said we should expect a visit. And lo, but didn't that visit come soon after that phone call, the knock on the front door of our small raised ranch, that very afternoon, knocked they did, so polite they were. But You know all about it because You know all. You saw it all. You were there, You're always there—everywhere, in my head and in my deeds, in my prayers and intercessions, in the sweat on my sheets, any action on my part already prefigured, a part of Your divine plan. Seems to me, now looking back, You might even have had some orchestrating role in it all. Something larger than my meager mind could comprehend. Perhaps somewhere in the back of my head, as they say, I was led, in fact, to act out this role. Programmed by My Creator. A willing servant, I. For who but You, after all, understands so well the ways and manner of temptation? That great serpent, he of the whisper and waggle, that blower of breezes that lifts the hem of a pretty plaid Sunday school dress and wafts toward a father's nose the siren scent of unbreached girlhood, he of the false promises, he of the great illusion, the king of lies, the grand seducer, that beast was created by You, after all, LORD. Your fingerprints are all over this family's house. She is our little girl. But she is, in the end, Your little girl. And that's what we will say to anyone who will listen: *Visited upon in her sleep.* And yet that fucking pig of South Carolina law enforcement said to his partner:

—*Wait, Ray, they got a name for that, what do they call that? A succubus?*

—*Nah, Mike,* said the other pig, a South Carolina nigger pig, standing up free and proud in his blue shirt sleeves, his muscley arms, dangling his shiny black night stick, shiny like his shiny shaved-bald eggplant head, standing in the doorway of our living room, inside our own home, in front of photos of our little girl. —*It's* incubus, *Mike, because the male ghost sticks it in, see; whereas the female ghost, she sucks it. Get it, "suck"? Think he's talking about an* incubus, *Mike.*

—*Aw, that's nice, Ray, got yourself a pneumonic device there. Well, big guy here can call it whatever he wants. His daughter keeps fucking up her story. Like she's reading a script. Says she bleeds 'cause she got stigmata from an angel's visitation. You ever heard of a stigmata staining a school seat like that, huh, big guy?*

I said I was going into that bedroom right that instant to talk to my little girl and to straighten this all out, and that's when the white pig broke my arm—on purpose, I do believe, LORD. He twisted me around in my own kitchen and put my wrist behind my back, up to my neck, up to where it shouldn't have gone.

—You're hurting me, officer, sir.

And I didn't mean to spit, but spit I did, and he pushed my arm higher, and the other pig tore my wrist-skin inside too-tight handcuffs, my arms bent back behind me at the elbow and up near my neck like ferocious wings, and then they yanked my arms down the wrong way, and that's when I both heard and felt the snap above my right forearm, my pitching arm, that All-American athletic talent You gave me, LORD, gone to rot right there with that one snap, that precious bone's break, and now all the poor thing does is hang loose like an empty shirt sleeve; no more fast balls from that one, no sir, LORD; pain beyond my poor power of description. And You know that a no-good arm is no good in Broad River.

And lo, would they have dispensed the same treatment and said all that accursedness to Joseph in regards about the Blessed Virgin, LORD? Her gravid womb, its blessed skin still miraculously intact, the mystery of that *sacred threshold* never breached. Would they have dragged Joseph of Nazareth—he who never breached that *sacred threshold*, he who stood aside for the immaculate cuckolding, that sterile yet staggering assignation— would they have dragged him on his knees across the linoleum floor of his own kitchen, pulled him up by his hair and ears to his Formica countertop, holding with their South Carolina pig hands his cheek against the dark brown glass of his microwave oven while they took turns striking and again striking the splintering bones of his shattered shins with their polished black clubs, striking him long after he swore he wouldn't try to run again, wouldn't try to kick again, wouldn't spit no more?

117

Would they have done such a thing to me if I was Joseph, O LORD? Tell me, would they have done? Even after I told them at my front door, responding to their polite-as-fuck-all knocking, before they pushed their way in and past me, breaching with their manly intention my own sacred threshold, even after I told them that I was at prayer just now and to excuse me from these legal matters of the world, these accusations wrongly issued? Polite, I was, even after they responded in the negative when I asked if they had obtained a search warrant. Would they have done? *Some mistake made somewhere, officers. I hereby solemnly promise to clear it all up A.S.A.P. My little girl got groined on the cross bar of her bike this weekend, that's all that mess on her seat was. But now that you mention it, officers, as regards what you report she was saying, we did—that is, her mama and me—hear ghostly noises in her bedroom last night. She wouldn't tell us what all it was about when we came knocking, so we tried to open the door but it wouldn't give and so we said, honey, open your door; let us in. But she had locked it against us. And we here in this house, officers, we respect a person's privacy. Didn't see or touch her again until this morning when she left for school. Before you come bringing all this foolishness to my door.*

And so we ask, LORD, her mama and me, who want to keep her with us, and us out of harm's way (for You know, as do I, what they do to you in here for this kind of thing), we ask You, nay beseech you, LORD, with all the angels and saints, we ask that our little girl, with the tattered and torn hem of her pretty plaid Sunday school dress, her missing skin, her breached threshold, her immaculate wound, we ask that she learn the lines we taught her. Express and annunciate the mystery of her own breached threshold. We have faith You will help us, LORD, her mama and me. And lo, when I think back to the boy I was with the All-American pitching arm, those dark days when I doubted not only my athletic talent, but my mind, my very thinking process itself, I recall, as I'm sure You recall, Ma saying all the time back then: *There's something wrong with the way*

118

you think, boy. Don't you come in this house thinking those thoughts.
And now, when she comes to Broad River for her visits, while
I wait, handicapped and helpless, in here for an answer to my
prayers, she says it again and again, words she seems to have
memorized. Sits across from me, she does, on the other side,
these benches cold and hard, this glass smeared with spit and
snot, the cameras always on, the redundant guards watching
our every move, and all the other visitors smoking 'cept for Ma,
her golden Bible in her gingham lap, her hands folded upon
that heavy book, her eyes unblinking, she, looking through the
smeared glass, says, *I'll always come visiting you, boy. But you can't
count on me forever. You gotta invite the LORD in. Open yourself to
his presence, boy. He the only visitor you ever gonna need. He the light.
He the cure. Let him in when he knocks, my son, invite him in for a
visit, and I swear, all the days of your life, you shall surely know peace.*

For the Running Man

Almighty LORD, Engineer of the universe, Author of all things, we praise you for the foresight to grant us legs for walking and with which we perambulate the regions of your creation, as we delight in moving about from place to place. We appreciate that our legs bend at the knees, allowing us to sit, or to crawl upon the ground when necessary, and to kneel, as when praying, or to retrieve personal objects we have dropped or to closer inspect natural and man-made phenomena. We pray that we will think of the miracle of legs the next time we see the man we refer to simply as "The Running Man," an individual who appears from time to time in our town and who is so named because we have never seen him not running, a man who is also never clothed in traditional running garb, who has elected to sport no athletic gear and whose shoes have not been constructed, as so many other runner's shoes are, by space-age materials. Remember, oh LORD, this fellow, whose reason for running hither and yon we know not, and guide our speculations so that they might honor rather than devolve into mockery; that is, let us not suppose that The Running Man is a few fries short of a Happy Meal, or that because, as it has been said, that he is a professor of mathematics, and therefore naturally eccentric, and also prevent us from ridiculing The Running Man's hair, LORD, as it is cut in an anachronistic bowl-type style and flops around as he jogs. And should we ever be tempted to mock the features of his face, which is sun-scorched and burdened with a potato-shaped nose, may we also remember the boys who ridiculed the prophet Elisha, who told him to "Go up, bald man! Go up!" and then You sent bears out of the woods to devour the boys, who thus learned their lesson the hardest way possible, which is to be eaten alive by a ferocious and very hungry creature. And so too preserve the knees of the Running Man, let him run long after his doctors warn him about stress fractures, and let us remember that he is ours, he belongs to us and to our town, and that as long as we have eyes to see and feet to carry us forward, we cheer him on, to whatever victories—if only within himself—to which he might lay claim.

For the Woman of a Certain Age Joining Match.com [again]

OH, MASTER OF THE HEART, Eros, Cupid, God of Many Names, Thou Fickle One, see fit to give this woman power to read between the lines, the gift of divinity, as she scrolls with studied nonchalance the men who grin at her from their little boxes. Allow her grace to skip the unshirted ones, the ones who are "just lookin' for a lady," the ones posed beside their cars, motorcycles, boats, lawn mowers. Strengthen her sight that she may divine faces behind sunglasses and baseball caps. Give her the gift of tongues that she may decipher their codes. Allow her not to linger on 50-year-olds who desire women only between the ages of 18-35, or men who claim themselves to be "cunning linguists." Let her gaze upon the red flags, oh LORD, and ignore them not lest she perish. Allow her to meet one, just one—is this asking too much, oh LORD my god?—who looks somewhat like his profile photo, who has not aged ten years in two minutes, who has not gained thirty pounds, who arrives on time and speaks not of his ex-wife. Still the men's tongues, oh LORD, and let them not utter the phrase, this is worse than going to the dentist, or why haven't you ever been married? Allow her the dignity to gaze beyond them and say nothing, to cough delicately into her hand, rather than cut them with her speech. Or make her fluent in the language of talk that is not too small, not too large, just right. We beseech you, oh LORD, give them common ground. Let them find one person, place, or thing on which they can land together and breathe. Allow the leave-taking to be sure, the utterance we should get together again be true. And if not, give her shoulders that shrug, a heart coated with Teflon. Please let her remember to cancel her membership before it automatically renews. We ask you this in the name of all that is holy and right. *Amen.*

For the Drivers of Tractor Trailers

Almighty and everlasting LORD, look with pity upon our roads, those networks of painted asphalt along which those among us have thoughtlessly discarded our cigarettes and cheeseburger wrappers and Skoal tins and cans of energy drink, not remembering or ever thinking of the engineers that subjected the concrete for our bridges to stress-testing in university laboratories or the sun-scorched workers who graded the asphalt or the goggled moms inhaling the chemical mist of our line painters. Let us keep in mind those who came before us, for whom travel was an arduous and generally unsafe enterprise, the trampled underfoot, the disease-ridden, the ice-burned, the fatigued, the saddle-sore. And, as we don our clothing and open our cereal boxes and unscrew the plastic tops of almond milk containers, let us remember that these things traveled to us from great distances, along roads, most likely in giant trucks piloted by men and women who spend their lives hauling our nation's products. And as we climb into our own vehicles and head out upon our roads, knit our hearts together in gratitude, and kindle not our rage, since it so often catches fire within us, not unlike a stack of wood we've doused in charcoal lighter when we feel wronged, when the cars in front of us fail to use a turn signal or pass slowly in the left lane. Let us not feel bullied by eighteen-wheelers or interpret their girth and swaying trailers and the deafening, impersonal drone of their engines—which are designed to travel a million miles—as an affront. Prevent us from cursing their drivers, who are, after all, people like us, men and women who have failed drug tests and who rub arthritic hands and need desperately to eliminate waste and smoke too much, those whose fathers and grandfathers drove trucks and who ferry shoes and clothing and fruits and vegetables and pickles and meats and electronics and soaps and milk and, remind us that as children each of these monstrosities were opportunities, back when we rode without booster chairs and never buckled in the back seat, enabling us to turn and watch everything we left behind unspooling and pumping our fists in a gesture that might have looked obscene but was a universal sign indicating we wanted a semi driver to pull the cord above their heads and toot their horns. Let us not forget, o LORD, that we loved horns, and were not ashamed to ask strangers to blow them, and that these good men and women might have been—who knows?—angels unaware.

For the Driver of the Oversized Load Escort Vehicle

O LORD, as the day meets the sun, will you not show Mercy on he of common employ and alleviate HeavyHaulers.com Driver #23, Mark Neblett of the overactive bladder that has plagued him as of late. Heavenly Father, this dark world is full of trials, but it is particularly dispiriting to have a teenage drugstore employee ask whether you need your adult diapers bagged.

And LORD, should you find it in your heart to be further clement, may Mark make it past exit 18b on I-95 without exasperation and accept with Compassion and Grace that for a reason still unknown to him—O! For the LORD's plan is Mysterious!—all motorized vehicles have always slowed to a halt around Mamaroneck and will continue to do so for all time.

And in your ever loving Mercy, LORD, will you also provide him with the strength to withstand his cravings for carbohydrate-rich and fatty foods because his wife, Debby, has been going to Curves a lot recently and might or might not be cheating on him with the District Manager at the Danbury Mall, and being an overweight divorcee wasn't part of the five-year financial plan Mark set up with that pleasant woman from H&R Block last month.

(Also LORD, if you could help him to request 'Balsamic *Vinegar*' and not 'Balsamic *Dressing*' if Rich insists on stopping at the Olive Garden again, because apparently 'Balsamic Dressing' is made with vegetable oil, which means extra fat.)

And in the dark hours between two and five p.m. when his blood sugar level is crashing and his eyelids long to close, will you not cast the mighty from their thrones, LORD, so that Mark may experience some upward mobility or maybe a promotion? At the very least, a little conjugal affection, so that he might set forth upon his tomorrows with a renewed sense of purpose. It could be a tongue kiss. That would be just fine.

It is in Mark's knowledge, LORD, that to drive the escort vehicle behind an Oversized Load is a humble and necessary and union-protected enterprise—but it is also known to Mark that his days are filled with tedium and debilitating regret, and that sometimes, the Oversized Vehicle's driver, Richard Musso, will put his blinker on for no reason and leave it on for seven exits and then haphazardly switch it off, and that gestures like this make Mark harbor spiteful thoughts against his neighbor.

(O, and LORD, Mark keeps forgetting to put ear plugs in his dopp kit, and the target audience of Motel 6 has changed some in the past years. Won't you guide him through the wilderness? Won't you protect Mark from the storm? Let him not be led into sleep deprivation and probable job loss, but rather to the "Personal Care" aisle of CVS where—Hark!—a ten-pack of ear plugs is available for $3.99.)

And in his darkest moments, when his lowly heart is full of scorn, when he has been staring at Rich's yellow "Oversized Load" banner for seven hours straight, when every under-exercised muscle in his infrequently touched body begins to twitch and his soul says, Lo! Mark! Abandon the Semi! Just take exit 3 up there and forever, pull away—May the Peace of the LORD enter him like a song, for O, the road is lengthy, and O, this life is long, but the All-Mighty's hand is with us in each happening. It is the force behind each wave. As it was in the beginning of the morning, may it not be forever. So help him, LORD.

For Those Perusing Souvenirs Sold in
Gas Stations or Truck Stops

Almighty FATHER, who is always in His house, remind us, whether we look upon these plastic trinkets as laughable trash, or gifts worthy of bestowing upon our loved ones, or glittering nonsense for our children to demand until we drag them screaming to the car, or part and parcel with the world of goods we could afford if only things had gone a little differently, that all of us are blessed in moments we remember the hours we have put between ourselves and our homes, and that these souvenirs, birthed in foreign lands by men and women with foreign lives to which we are afforded no insight by the products of the labor that keeps their families housed and fed, these souvenirs of no place in particular, that will be the same in Wells, Nevada or Welcome, Minnesota, cannot tell us how far we have gone, or have yet to go. The remembering must be ours, however else we choose to marvel before these shelves.

Remind us, who live in the world of things manifest by infallible will, that the flotsam shit cast over the retail network of gas stations and truck stops is much further from home than we ourselves, and will never be returned, because it does not know its distance, and cannot tell us of the days spent in the dark of shipping containers aboard thrumming freighters churning the face of the waters, and should we ever purchase one or many of these souvenirs, and invite them into our houses, let them not bring with them the wet slap of waves, the violent rocking of storms, the stinging brine, but simple hours, safe in our cars, the fuzz of the radio as the interstate draws each station further away, and the brittle scrub-brush on the gravel shoulder of a course, charted and paved for every journey.

For the Tin Man

Eternal God, You who govern all things in heaven and on earth, watch over us and guide us as we attempt to traverse the hectic and congested sidewalks of the metropolis in which we have made our homes and lives. Enable us through your beneficence to slip easily and speedily between the sluggish walkers, window-shoppers, and disoriented tourists, whose sudden and unexpected halts may cause us to collide with them, or to halt, ourselves, thus creating a domino effect of abrupt stoppage and/or collision all the way up the block. Grant us grace and compassion as we maneuver around these lost souls, for they are not lost in the Kingdom of the LORD. Give us the strength to tolerate the Tin Man, whose recent presence at one particular intersection, and the subsequent crowding of onlookers, has rendered the sidewalk more impassible than ever. Watch over the Tin Man, o LORD, as he sets up his daily busking bucket and assumes the posture and immobility of a statue while tourists scurry to his side to pose for innumerable photo ops. Guide the Tin Man, Almighty God, as he subsequently launches into a Michael Jackson impersonation, a single sequined glove upon his silver wrist, silver lips pursed into what we imagine must be some form of seductive scowl. Look with gentleness upon the Tin Man as he pops his hips and glides backwards across the tarred and gum-stained sidewalk in a rough impression of the Moonwalk, forcing a clearing of the crowd and sometimes, in so doing, crowding us sheer off the curb and into the street. Assist us, merciful God, in appreciating the fluidity and elegance of the Tin Man's body as he executes Michael Jackson's trademark moves, for surely we could not hope to conduct our bodies with such natural grace even in the privacy of our own bedrooms, to say nothing of performing before scores of strangers on a high-traffic corner of a bustling metropolis. We pray for the health of the Tin Man and for the nontoxicity of the thick silver paint which he has applied to every exposed centimeter of his skin, and perhaps the unexposed centimeters as well. Grant us the restraint to keep from muttering that while Michael Jackson's own pigmentation did raise certain questions among both admirers and detractors, it was definitely never silver, and that the Tin Man ought to choose whether he wants to be a Tin Man or Michael Jackson. Let us not heckle the Tin Man, Heavenly Father, with suggestions that we have seen better Tin Men and better Michael Jackson Impersonators elsewhere. Let us refrain from mentioning that we have seen better buskers in general, for instance the levitating turban-wrapped sheik in the pedestrian mall in Freiburg, or the Marilyn Monroe lookalike in Los Angeles who stood over a wind vent for three straight hours batting down her skirt while maintaining an impressively coquettish half-smile. Preserve us from deliberating too long why we stayed on that Los Angeles street corner the full three hours, for the LORD works in mysterious ways. Bless and keep the Tin Man, o God, and watch over him when we in our weakness are more forthcoming with our cameras than our coin purses. In your infinite wisdom and grace, LORD, let us not forget that when the Tin Man assumes the frozen posture of the statue, we become aware of our own free-swinging limbs; when he gyrates and Moonwalks, we become aware of the corporeal possibilities of Man as created in Your image; when we behold his painted flesh, we become aware of our own comparatively open pores, and so in spite of the worsening of the already abundant and delay-causing crowds that impede our passage through the city, bless him, o LORD, and keep him.

For Flight Attendants Giving Safety Speeches

Forgive us, O LORD, for not looking, for averting our eyes, for opening the Sky Mall magazine even though we couldn't truly be said to be interested in Roland the Gargoyle Sculptural Rain-spout or the Tranquil Sounds Oxygen Bar. Forgive us too for scrolling through our phones and powering up our electronic readers or twisting the plastic doohickeys above our heads to decrease the stale-smelling airflow pouring onto our faces. We are ashamed, LORD, to watch these ladies—and yes, LORD, those attendants who are women are all ladies, by which we mean strong and selfless arbiters of hospitality—as they do the thing they are, by law, required to do, and the thing that they, in fact, are paid to do, which is to deliver pertinent information concerning what nobody wants to think about, which is what to do and how to proceed if the giant vehicle we all will soon ride into the sky somehow malfunctions, or a Canadian goose flies into a turbine, and pilots are forced to crash land into earth or water. And while we fear dying, LORD, the truth of the mat-ter is that we also fear that we will be caught watching the At-tendants during their speeches, that our fellow passengers will notice our forward-looking gaze and cast judgment upon us, because we don't want to give the impression that we are new enough to air travel to not ignore the safety speech. It's not that we don't think the safety speech is important, LORD; we do. And it's not that the safety speech itself doesn't ignite the fuse of our fear, which, in moments like these, can be palpable, as we admit to having faith in the ability of a giant winged capsule launch us and other strangers to a cruising altitude of 33,000 feet, and despite knowing words like "turbine" and "wingspan," we don't have any idea how this machine works, and why—like cars steering off embankments—more planes simply don't fall out of the sky. We also don't know what our Flight Attendant is thinking, of if she feels awkward, or if feeling awkward is old hat, and thus is not awkward at all. We don't know how many

130

times she had to practice before she memorized the speech in its entirety or, as seems to be the case nowadays, mastered the timing required to synchronize the buckling and pulling taut of the safety belt while a pre-recorded voice describes its fastening, or the placing over her head the oxygen mask with the instructions to do so, and though we recognize that there's a sort of off-putting, automated quality to most of these speeches/ pantomiming, we definitely notice when the actor—that is, our Attendant—takes the role seriously, by which we mean that she doesn't look bored but pleasantly engaged with this activity or that she never gives up trying to maintain eye contact with the uninitiated few who are actually paying attention, as this imbues her with a kind of authority that, whether we take the time to recognize it or not, allows us to be more comfortable, to settle back in our seats, and subsequently more likely to stow our electronic equipment during takeoff and landing, as we would hate to disappoint someone with such an authoritative yet convivial presence. Furthermore, LORD, protect our Attendant, post-safety-speech, for that is when many of us—and we're not proud of this, but it happens—will eyeball her, will note the hip-hugging skirt, the collared shirt open enough to reveal an expanse of neck flesh, and the absence of a ring on her left hand, and embark upon a detailed fantasy in which we might, in some alternate universe, have occasion to meet her later at an airport bar, and saying something like, "Hey, I remember you," and "You were the Attendant on my flight," to which she'd maybe raise an eyebrow while snatching a complimentary pretzel from wax-paper-lined basket, and say something like, "Yep. That's me," and although she's suffered this same rigmarole on many occasions, has been approached by her share of admirers, or those who are merely curious about the life of a Flight Attendant—a life that is, let's be honest, so often and rightly romanticized—she'd say "Sure" when we ask if we might buy her a drink—a vodka tonic, or another glass of Merlot—and if we're lucky (and, as you know, LORD, in our imaginations we always

131

are), we might hear stories about the places our Attendant has visited, how she once listened to a symphony at the Singapore Botanic Garden or tried mulukhiyah in Dubai or shopped for trinkets in Abidjan's Treshville market, and that her favorite place to stay is the Kempinski Hotel in Budapest, one of the cheapest luxury hotels in the world, where she's quite fond of following a full body massage with a dinner of Black Spaghetti with Fried Seafood and Tomatoes. Of course, it's not all glamor and glitz. There was that one time when the turbulence was so bad over the Atlantic that our Attendant—bless her heart—had to shut her eyes and bite her lip and think about the pale blue water lit by lantern light at a Tahitian bungalow. And maybe she tells the story of the spilled coffee. Or how, in some countries, when you touch down and pick up passengers, it's totally legit to walk up and down the aisle with a can of air freshener, to reduce the odor of bodies that consume pungent herbs and rarely bathe. Maybe she tells us how she hates it when travelers ask for Diet Coke, because the drink's particular fizz takes three times longer to pour than the average soft drink. Maybe she tells us that she has a son who dropped out of community college and is touring Europe in a hardcore band. Maybe she has a daughter studying Human Nutrition at a State University. Maybe her husband killed himself, or left her, or died of a pulmonary embolism, or still loves her, or never existed. Maybe our Attendant is lonely or fine with being alone, or perfectly happy, or jaded, or vengeful, or taking online courses so she can finish a Bachelor of Arts in Religious Studies. Maybe she imagines, during each and every takeoff, that the Boeing 787 in which she travels, and which is the first line of aircraft to be built with composite materials, will take a sudden nose-dive, and that on this day she and the passengers whom she attends will be incinerated by a giant ball of flame. Maybe. The truth is, LORD, we don't know. And, in all likelihood, we never will. And probably, we shouldn't. Because we're pretty sure that the last thing our Attendant wants, LORD, and of this we can be quite certain, is to be the subject of our assumptions, or to come alive, as it were, in our imaginations. So please, LORD, avert our gaze. Let us not order Diet Coke. And, as we depart, let us thank our Attendant for her service, and wish her a heart-felt and sincere goodbye.

For the Newly Minted Ph.D. in English Literature

O FATHER, merciful and benevolent, please watch over the newly minted Ph.D. graduate in English Literature who knows not yet how cruel the world will become. Stay with him through his travails involving the teaching jobs he coveted but wasn't awarded, as well as the disappointment and bitterness toward the second tier colleges he lowered himself to apply to but that ultimately rejected him. Be especially vigilant, O LORD, during the bleak months after his doctoral thesis on Homelessness in the Novels of Charles Dickens fails to find a publisher and he flirts with the notion of self-publishing for the sake of "getting it out there." Guide him through the depression of taking an office job, the same kind of clerical position he held before he entered the Ph.D. program, as well as the shame of reading obscure Knut Hamsun novels in his car on his lunch break, fuming over the lack of interest of his heathenish colleagues in the delicious fact that Nabokov mistakenly has two parallel streets in Phoenix running perpendicular in *Lolita*. Empower him, BLESSED, to use his learning to navigate the hardships of his day-to-day existence: when no one readily sees the obvious connection between Tolstoy's fetishizing peasantry and Melville's obsession with whaling; when a colleague mistakes the paragraph retyped from *The Golden Bowl* and tacked up in his cubicle as a bit from an episode of *The Simpsons*; when the girl in accounting looks at him askance after he utters the Joycean quip about having a potato in his pocket. Lead him out of temptation, LORD, when the newly minted Ph.D. graduate in English Literature's faith begins to waver and he downloads law school applications. Show him the path of the righteous that have traveled before him and redeem in his eyes those Ph.D. graduates in English Literature who found fulfillment in their calling as astrologers, booksellers, ghostwriters, and henna tattoo artists. Let it be written here and forever after that the enormous sums spent on a Ph.D. in English Literature are more easily justified at enrollment than they ever will be upon graduation. *Amen.*

For the Translator

...or traitor, if You like, for she's known by many names. O God, may Your fountain be gold for this lilt language warrior. She is silent, she silences. Righteously she adds and subtracts Your earth-torn timbre. God, give her the strength to barter fair contracts, let her be not interned in nameless servitude. Nay! Let her name grace the front page, even. Rejoice in the translator who is equal font to the author—for sure, his work is noble, but Jesus, what justice is there in his hulk eclipsing her gorgeous form? Her transcendent text! O Lord, pry open Your holy heart, for her text is a blessing to Your loyal servant trapped in the gray, single cell of the target language, rising above the rape and babble of slanderers who would call her work mere reproduction. Sweet Christ, she is both nimble and faithful, transforming strange and similar lands. She travels in ships, in space, in womb. She ghosts, she channels, she dissects. She is Your lively margin and Your lettered center. O breathtaking, O brave her interventions! In Thy name, she creates a body akin to pure. We beseech Thee: let her be loved as she so loves the word—that howl-thrash, that contingent wreck in which she lives, an eye wise and unsettling.

Three Prayers for Artists

For Sandwich Artists

Almighty Branch Manager, please gaze favorably from your franchise in the sky and bestow a satisfactory employee rating upon this starving sandwich artist who has not only affirmed his commitment to unironically following the corporate spokesperson on Twitter but also vowed to serve the freshest $5 foot longs imaginable. Give him Adderall, Ativan, Klonopin, Vicodin, and whatever other street drugs it takes for him to make a decent sandwich on an annual salary that's much lower than an actual artist's annual salary; and strengthen all of us sub club customers in our resolve to trust in the wisdom of high quality produce, excellent customer service, and low operating costs. May we all eat fresh in the service of slim waistlines and the LORD; in Jared's name we pray. *Amen.*

For Con Artists

Oh God, great private eye in the sky, we respectfully ask that you stop tailing us and, moreover, we pray for your forgiveness. Oh LORD, we admit that the good Spirit has not always guided us, and that we've spent decades picking pockets, cheating tax collectors, and fleecing rubes with everything from fool's gold necklaces to timeshares on the moon. True, but all that badness is behind us. Now we're asking you for your almighty assistance: it is our great pleasure, LORD, to pray to you and present a modest business proposal for your consideration. It is our great pleasure, LORD, to pray to you and ask you to assist us in the transfer of eleven million, five hundred thousand U.S. dollars to your bank account in heaven. Heavenly Father, should you decide to render your services in this regard you would be paid 33% of the total funds for your assistance. Reply with a sign if you are willing to work with us. *Amen.*

For Conceptual Artists

Oh God, we are running out of ideas! We just realized the concept of the universe is the only concept! Now we are echeloning our concepts and acknowledging you as the fundamental one, oh LORD, but we'd like to note that the first word in "concept" is "con," which seems suitable given the long con you've pulled on the universe with your continuous silence. Oh, we are listening to you listening to us listening to you. Oh, this is a portrait of you because we say so. It is a diamond-encrusted skull: a memento mori for an immortal. It is a sculpture of a urinal in a museum somewhere in heaven. It is a chair where no one sits, next to the definition of the word "chair." It is also prayer without a prayer. *Amen.*

For the Hostess on the Eve of an Ill-Conceived Party

Oh LORD, Purveyor of goodness, Keeper of light, have mercy on a woman who is gripped with the unholy impulse to invite 60 people into her small home for the department's end-of-year party. Understand that she is addled and knows not whereof she speaks. If in Your omnipotence, You cannot restrain her tongue, nor instill Sense into her menopausal brain, show mercy on her and give her the number for catering. Give her Wit to navigate the maze of bureaucratic forms she must complete, and give her Strength to withstand the unforeseen needs of her Guests. Grace her with the miracle of Cash and Carry, the multitude of paper goods and plastic cups, napkins and compostable forks. Bestow the wisdom of Cleaning Ladies who gift her with Resolve to wipe out the abomination of cat vomit. Send forth the Green Thumb Landscaping crew, who will scorch the earth of any weed. Send thy neighbor to help her construct Badminton where before no Badminton existed. Push her chairs to the corner of the dining room and remove all Evidence of medication and bodily secretion. Oh Compassionate One, if you can, please, oh God, call up the sun so the Guests do not cluster in her tiny kitchen, but instead mill about pleasantly on her deck. Yet please temper the sun so the Guests will not complain it's too hot. Compel the Guests to be cheerful, to play Badminton, to get along, to behave. Restrain the meat of their tongues from uttering Gossip, but if this prove too onerous for even thou, oh LORD, at least let not one person ask a work-related question or offer a problem for her to solve, okay, just for these few hours, *capiche?* May the spanakopita be warm and the hummus cold, and may the gluten intolerant find their way to the rice crackers. May the lactose intolerant be satisfied with the dolmas, and the vegans ingest the falafel. May the little children find not the one breakable object she neglected to hide. May the evening end naturally, the Guests leaving with whispered expressions of gratitude and Awe. Instill the Hostess, oh LORD, with the wherewithal to clean up quickly, immediately, before the mess settles in to breed. By grace of Your infinite Wisdom, allow the sun to dip behind clouds and cast Thine golden light into her rooms as she finishes. Allow her this moment of Satisfaction, her thought: *well, that wasn't so bad.* We ask you this truly in the name of Martha Stewart and the grandmothers on high, may it be so, *Amen.*

Prayer: Friday Night at Hot Slice

On this day the musicians enter to muted applause.

O God almighty and everliving, you have summoned us in this pizza joint to a goodly fellowship of rock. Bless our lead singer A., may his words please thee and the girls in the mosh pit, may his worship of his own image detract not from our labors. By your spirit, may the PA be grounded and his rosy lips not crack and sizzle in currents electrical. Let him muss his hair up a little and please, LORD, let him lose the scarf. Let not his stoned monologue last night about why Paul was better than John have strained his voice, so that his word may be truly preached and truly heard, even in the back, where the A&R rep would be standing, if an A&R rep ever came to one of our shows.

Almighty and evelasting God, give grace to our drummer B., grant him the strength to tune his heads for once in his life, let him not insist it sounds good either way, for it does not, even his girlfriend agrees. Father of us all, let him imbibe just enough to curb his anxiety, yet not so much that he is insensible. Let him remember that one fill he always blows, and grant him the strength to recall which song we are playing all the way through. May thy spirit lend him the imagination not to use the word "amazeballs" again, dear God, in the name of your son Jesus Christ our LORD, we are so sick of "amazeballs," and there are no other decent drummers in this town, so please, we beseech thee, truly we do.

O LORD our Governor, let not our bassist C. talk to her mother on the phone before the show. Save her from this bitterness, so that she might not inform the audience that this one is going out to that bitch, her mother, and then turn her master volume up to ten. Father of our LORD Jesus Christ, may the spirit of thy wisdom prevent our bassist from bringing the fretless bass, for she is not Jaco Pastorius, headband and turtleneck notwithstanding; let us not take Your good name in vain pointing out that we are a rock band, a goddam rock band, see, there, we took your name in vain, such is the depth of our suffering. Let us, O God, remember not to ask our bassist if she is "on the rag," because that did not go over too well last time.

Grant, Heavenly Father, our lead guitarist D. the ability to recall that he was hired as, in fact, a guitarist. Let him not proclaim himself "lead synthesist" again on this day; indeed, let him not bring his so-called "keys" to this gig at all. And if, most merciful God, your grace is inadequate to prevent this insult to Your Holiness, then grant us the courage not to "accidentally" "forget" his "synth rig" in the gas station parking lot. O most gracious LORD, let the guitarist's work friends not attend tonight, for they are alcoholic doucheclowns. If they must come, beseech them not to request "Free Bird" and, should this misfortune nevertheless befall us, grant D. the strength not to try to play it.

Look with mercy, O God our blessed Father, upon this band tonight. Make our instruments the instruments of your peace. Let the sound guy not hog the take from the door. Let us tip the bartenders well, for they could make our evening really, really shitty if they wanted to. Let those musicians who wish to be fellated or fingered kindle affections with those inclined to finger or fellate, so that they may call Your blessed name to Heaven in the alley behind the firehouse. We beseech thee, Almighty God, not to let our shit get stolen. Protect our strings against breakage, our amps against electrical shorts, our songs against repetition and cliché. Bless, O LORD, these gifts so that we may use them in your service again soon, the third Thursday in March, in fact, opening for Roxy Barnes and the Doubtin' Cowboys at Trendz, hope y'all can make it, we got tee shirts in the back, please "like" us on facebook, thanks and good night. Amen.

For the Reunion of the White Stripes

Your name, Shaddai, says Dr. Donne, means "spoyle and violence and depredation." Who can argue with that? You sat back,
obese on the manna of heaven, as Jack White disbanded the
White Stripes in 2011. You no doubt thought, as You tend to
think, that earth needed more depredation, more blight, more
Beiber. We are willing to overlook Your overlooking Beiber if
You resolve to reunify Jack and Meg. Consider it Your divine
duty, a making-up for all the fucking-up You've done since Gen-
esis—for allowing Henry Kissinger to live and John Updike to
die, for instance. For populating America with the diabetical
obese who crowd aisles. Granted, Jack is notoriously difficult.
Not Axl-Rose-difficult, but still—difficult. Narcissism, ego-infla-
tion, solipsism—all regrettable but necessary side-effects of genius. As you know, Great One. Now, as we understand it, Meg
didn't want to be in the Stripes any longer. Meg had anxiety.
Meg was shy. Meg was exhausted after the *Icky Thump* tour in
'07. So it seems as if Meg is the culprit who requires Your ab-
racadabra. We love the Raconteurs, do not misunderstand us.
We can, however, do without the Dead Weather. And Jack as a
solo act, with his alternating male/female accompaniment and
blue-hued aesthetic—well, let's just say it all rather lacks the ban-
tam bravado and stripped-down, red-white-and-black sublimity
of the White Stripes. And—we're sorry—but another Black Keys
album does not compensate for no more albums by the Stripes,
try as Dan Auerbach will to rip off Jack's mojo. Furthermore,
when Jack was growing up Catholic in Detroit he seriously considered becoming a priest to praise You. That didn't work out,
thank You, but he considered it, which is more than most of
us do for Your bestial Self. Jack's artistic integrity is unassail-
able; we needed to hear what he said about Ashley Simpson
in the pages of *Rolling Stone* back in '05, after *Get Behind Me
Satan* came out. (And don't take that title as an insult; after all,
Satan is Your handiwork, and some of us even suspect you're

the same person. Or thing, whatever.) The point is: we need the White Stripes as antidote to all the toxic and shit-stupid music polluting our airwaves. This is a reasonable request; stop Your stalling. We're not asking you to paint the moon with rainbows (though our city of Boston would welcome that). Meg is waiting. Get going.

For Faithless Wives, on the Nightly Removal of Prosthetic Limbs

O LORD Who is closer to us than our next breath; Who is so enmeshed in our being that we would sooner be separated from our very pulse; Who shouts instruction through His vessels in the pulpit, speaks sage encouragement through ages and pages of texts too voluminous to read, and whispers secret wisdom in a still, small voice that we hear in our innermost ears, but which most of us think originates a little to the right of the belly, we thank You for Your passionate, even obsessive interest in our minutest thoughts, motives, and actions.

But I can't do it like this anymore, LORD.

I know we're supposed to pray to You in the plural to show that we're one body, Your body on earth. I, more than anyone, should understand the idea of one body being plural. You know what I'm talking about, LORD—my right hand is buried beneath a baseball diamond up north, my tongue clogged that toilet at church, and my left leg is fertilizing the grass in the backyard. And yet the more plural I become, the more alone I feel, even though I'm never, technically, alone anymore.

The only time I can sense Your presence is when I'm shedding more of me.

I'm not complaining. I'm not asking You to do anything for me. It's the woman You gave me I'm worried about. She was there when I kicked the dog. But she says it wasn't really a kick. She says it wasn't *supposed* to be scratching at the sofa as we sat together doing our daily devotions, that it was righteous of me to nudge it with my left foot—*nudge it*; her words—and that sometimes dogs just whimper when they've been corrected by their masters. She insists that the dog was not avoiding me any more than usual the week after, and that even if it was, it was no message from You about the way sin separates a man from God.

She hasn't left me five minutes to myself, five minutes with You, since she found me in the tub, the saw still in my hand, my leg, calf-to-foot, on the blood-smudged bathroom tiles. Worse, I think she's beginning to suspect that my tongue might not have had to come out, that I might not have babbled like the heathen at that healing service, that maybe I only went to third base with that girl at church camp back in junior high as an excuse to chop my hand off in front of her. She seems to think I'm looking for reasons to sin.

Looking to sin—that would be a good excuse for gouging out an eye. Right, LORD?

We'll see (ha ha). I'm not done looking for ways to do Your will, yet. For example, here I am praying to You as though You don't already know all of this. It's like my mind won't accept Your omniscience. From what I hear, lobotomy is as simple as sliding something flat and slim under an eyelid and up toward the brain.

But I have to tread carefully (also ha ha—I only have one leg!). My wife says if she sees me within reach of a sharp object, the next bodypart I'll lose will be her. You commanded me to leave my parents and cleave unto her and become one flesh. I'm also hoping to have a son one day, so that I might raise him to do Your will, as I have done. It's not like she's been letting me cleave unto her since the thing with my leg, but I can't exactly turn her into a phantom limb.

I'm asking You to forgive her, LORD. Each night, as she reads my scarred stumps with her fingers, she beseeches a god that I don't recognize to stop giving me signs.

For Very Thirsty Souls Who Are Out of Beer After the Liquor Stores Have Closed

O Father of mercies and God of all comforts, our only help in time of need: We humbly beseech thee to provide for us just one more beer. Look upon us with thy mercy; for surely our own mortal eyes have been too weak to see the Miller Lite logo hidden behind the milk jug. Surely in your infinite abundance, O LORD, you will lead our erring hand to the crisper, wherein we forgot we had stashed away a bottle of Milk Stout, or even just a lowly can of PBR. O Father, preserve us from the temptation to drink from the bottle of Ouzo that some joker gifted us at the White Elephant Christmas exchange; O LORD please spare us from having to drink that weird gooseberry flavored ale that our friends left here after their stay and that has gone unopened for many seasons now. LORD, if there be beer, then let us by the good grace of thy unwavering affection find it now for the love of you; or else please give us the patience, the good humor, and the steadfast temper to endure these infernally lingering party guests with nothing but a glass of champagne which, O LORD, is not to say that we are turning away the good fruits and beverages of thy vines but rather, O LORD, that it tries the patience of thy humble servant mightily to hear these endless stories about the twins and their diaper mishaps without a brew in hand Jesus Christ Dear Father Dear Holy Father Our LORD. In thy good time, restore our refrigerators to full and our glasses to overflowing and enable us to live our lives, O God, without the absence of one of thy most precious gifts. This we do pray, in the name of hops and yeast and dry malt, for one more beer, *AMEN*.

147

For Those Currently Much Drunker Than They Meant To Get

Dear LORD of Restraint and Common Sense—Going back in time and not having that third complimentary cocktail would have been a good idea but going back in time, as we understand the laws of your earthly kingdom, is not an option, and so here we are, drunker than we meant to be. Protect us, oh LORD, from saying things that we will regret later, no matter how honest or civil these things now seem. Forgive us, oh LORD, with enjoying the taste of margaritas instead of paying attention to the increasingly impaired mental condition and physical abilities of our bodies, which, we realize, are living temples to your creation, oh LORD. Deliver us from the other person at this party who also got drunker than they meant to get and do not let us share a cab back to Brooklyn with them for we both have a history of making out with each other when we are drunk and we really don't have the time for that kind of shit anymore. We are not getting any younger, LORD. Amen.

For Aging Rock Stars

Almighty God, who is the most almighty and godly God ever, and who undoubtedly knows a thing or two about what it is to be revered and worshiped by the general public, we beseech Thee to shower Thy blessings upon all aging rock and roll celebrities who still trod the Earth, like dinosaurs, in the twilight years of their fame. Console them, O LORD, as they enter unrecognized, alone, at night, a Winn-Dixie in the dim suburbs of a ruined and forsaken Southern town; give them the strength to bear themselves with dignity as they push a rattling shopping cart down the breakfast cereal aisle and not one person—not one!—stops to ask them for a photograph or autograph or even to just say hello. Fortify them when, near a chartered bus in the parking lot of a mid-sized urban theatre prior to a show with their new solo-venture Americana folk-fusion band, they encounter concert-goers arriving on electric scooters, or shuffling with difficulty up to the ticket windows with the aid of aluminum walkers and canes, some of them dragging behind them small canisters of oxygen. Fill Your aging rock stars with compassion when they see these same long-time fans attempting to shimmy in the aisles during a mid-concert Gambian-infused blues number, only to fall back into their seats trembling and gasping for air: for these are their true admirers, the ones who brave night-time driving and occasional incontinence to attend their shows, even when no one else is buying their new solo-venture recordings—and what, by the way, is wrong with people these days that they don't appreciate musical innovation? Huh, O God? Huh? Grant them, too, Your ancient rock stars, the strength to ignore the drunken woman jumping up and down on her seat in the balcony section, young enough to be their granddaughter, who repeatedly yells for them to play "Stairway to Heaven," even though they never, ever played that song—that was another band from the seventies who played that song, you ignorant, drunken girl. Get down off your seat, you stupid child! And at the end, O LORD, when they stand panting before a mirror in an over-lit backstage dressing room bracing themselves for a ten-minute encore medley of greatest hits, and they see, O God, their ridiculously long, tangled gray hair, and their paunchy belly extruding above the waistline of their tight black jeans, and their wrinkled, leathery, drug-and-alcohol-scored face, dabbed now with a little rouge at the cheek-bones—help them, merciful God, help them not to succumb to despair, not to think to themselves, "What has become of me and my life?," but rather, to find deep within themselves the power to return to face their poor, decrepit fans, and to attempt to rouse in them the same passion and joy they once inspired. And as they mount the stairs to the stage, almighty God, the stairs that grow higher and more perilous with every passing year, and they hear the crowd stomping and clapping and shouting their name, and they feel a sudden tightness in their chest below their ribcage, and—Holy Christ, are they having a heart attack? Now? Right here on these fucking steps on the way to their encore? You wouldn't do that, would you God? Not here, not now. Not when the tour's almost over. Would You? Show a little pity, for Christ's sake. Show some love. Carry them up, dear God. Carry them up one last time into the light, into the embrace of their screaming, arm-waving fans, so that they might all relive together, if only for an instant, if only for tonight, the golden thoughtless bliss of their youth.

For the Department Store Santa

Pity the Department Store Santa, God. His shift is long, the line to sit on his lap unending, and he's not looking so hot. Might be that he's gearing up for a migraine, God, a big one, which to us embattled Department Store Christmas Shoppers sounds like a special slice of hell. Consider the continuous loop of treacly carols piped over the mall's PA, singing chipmunks and jingling bells banging about inside his skull, or the colored lights festooning the enormous polyurethane fir tree and how they must for him glow ominously, casting unholy haloes that trail across his vision. Grant him mercy, God. His face has broken out in a rash, perhaps a reaction to the glue he uses to affix his beard, and we bet his arms and legs itch too, are probably covered with hives birthed by the red polyester costume that looks nothing like velvet or wool. His vinyl boots—which don't even vaguely resemble leather—are scuffed and cracked, and provide him very little arch support, but his job is to sit, after all. The Department Store Santa squints against the discomfort and growing pain, but he still smiles, God. The Department Store Santa still smiles.

Let's face it: his is not a job we would choose for ourselves, but he serves a purpose. We appreciate his and our shared culpability in the lies we tell our children (whom we spoil, we admit, when we allow ourselves through you to be honest). That Santa is real, the physical spirit of Christmas and embodiment of altruism (as long as you're on the right list). And so on. We imagine with both awe and distaste his plight. Our youngest children are terrified of him. Our kids slightly older, say five or six or perhaps an unusually gullible or unimaginative or unobservant eight year old, are beginning to suspect something fishy and scrutinize this man's loose beard, how his eyebrows are black rather than gray, and that he doesn't know—despite the fabled twice-checked list—anyone's names. Our eldest stopped believing years ago but are expected to play along—they're bored and annoyed and roll their eyes and sadistically leap into the Department Store Santa's lap and grind their pointy tailbones into his thigh, punishing him instead of their overworked, underappreciated mothers wielding cameras who ask/plead/scold/threaten their children to smile, mothers whose entire sense of self-worth is at the moment invested in making *this* the perfect Christmas, already constructing *just* the right wording for the post they'll put on facebook later that evening, something like, Well, the whole fam finally made it to see Department Store Santa (god bless that poor man :))—NOW it feels like Christmas! Even if it isn't true. But make our hearts and minds *believe* that it's true, God. Preserve us from distrust, from malicious speculation, from suspicious questions like, who *is* this guy, anyway? Who would *choose* this job? Was he laid off? Fired? An alcoholic, maybe a closet pederast? Does the Department Store Santa get *his* jollies from dandling kids from his knee? He's diabetic, right? Got to be. He certainly doesn't look healthy. Or for that matter jolly. He's squinting, rubbing his temples. What the hell does he do for the rest of the year, anyway? Practice his ho ho ho?

We're bitter, God. We know. Redeem us, then, these Department Store Shoppers before you, driving the world economy since Thanksgiving. We propel the retail sector into the black while slowly shuffling through this unending line, clutching the sweaty hands of our spoiled children. There's something sordid about the whole thing, isn't there? Christmas—what it's become. Santa and his list, tallying up all our small acts, entering them into their respective columns, naughty or nice. Gifts or coal, kids—what'll it be? Heaven or hell?

No wonder this crisis of faith, God. You're an abstraction we pay lip service to, God, but your infinite grace and wisdom can't compete with the loot of Christmas morning (which, fyi, is still seven shopping days away). Maybe we're asking the wrong questions. Are we? By standing in this God-forsaken line (we're not, in this instance, using your name in vain, oh LORD, only making a point), have we turned away from *your* gifts? The impermanent bobbles that we teach our bratty children to ask Santa for—are these gifts solely to dull the existential dread that is the curse for turning away, for a failure to believe, a failure to suspend disbelief? Are we making too big a deal out of this? God, forgive us. Behold us, visit us, guide us. Give us the right questions to ask. Show us the way.

The line is moving, but slowly. Department Store Santa grips his head and gazes dumbly at a red-faced toddler screeching in his lap while we wait, inching past the cottony swaddles of polyester puff vaguely reminiscent of snow, the dancing plastic candy canes bedecked with glittery red stripes, and cardboard cutouts of poorly painted elves more creepy than merry-looking. Is this freedom, God? Independence and liberty? Jesus, his New Covenant, the most democratic and *American* of religions—he's our excuse to worship the ego, why we're drawn in the first place to this nice/naughty dichotomy of Jolly Saint Nick (whom, by the way, God, perhaps could use a touch more mercy. See how he's cradling his neck, how his smile's slipped, as has his beard—a child might notice, after all, and wonder). He's not The Santa but A Santa, a Department Store Santa, a paltry representation of an imaginary man whom in either your wisdom or disregard you've allowed to supplant your only begotten son.

We're still not asking the right question, God, are we? For the proper blessing. It's now impossible to deny and ignore that the Department Store Santa suffers, before us all, from intense pain. He can no longer hide it, and grips his head in both hands, eyes shut, and moans. It's terrible to watch, but what do we do? How do we act? This isn't part of the script, of our agreement. Whether the right question or not, one of our children,

153

still young enough to be frightened and believe, asks, "Mommy, what's wrong with that man?" What indeed, God?

For the Non-Participant Audience Members of *The Price is Right*

BLESSED LORD: The time has come, we the congregation pray, to bestow upon thy flock the long-pined manna of yore, yet contemporized, accessorized, blessed with clear-coat and prices right, which—enjoyed first most in remembrance of thee, preceding thy awaited revenant, after taxes—delivers us from the toils of our daily walk. This we ask but for our Christian names to resound as the trumpets once did throughout Jericho, destroying metaphorical walls of covetousness, for if fulfilled of our every earthly wish, would we not then become empty decanters to be brimmed over with thy holy spirit? Who at this time has many many thumbs and is beholden to the desire of vainglory? Surprise, O God, it is us, thy frustrated and uncalled dominion. Look with inimitable compassion upon all us seated here, name-tagged and compelled to clap, a blur of faces whirred across a screen, some having allocated five sick days for travel, spotting thy star in the West and hastening without thought to worship thee there. How can one turn away from hearts such as these? You who became poor for our sake, that we might be made rich through your poverty, although let us get real for one moment, Dear Father, thy ever-watchful audience seems to have pulled up a few pages short on the being made rich clause. Wherefore art our Plinko chips? What fabulous trip to Las Vegas awaits us? We beseech thee on occasion of such bountiful loot splayed here before thy restless children, testing us, it so seems, as you once did the Son of Man for forty days among the wilderness, though for He Who Art No Joke you simply dangled rocks and bread, and for us mortal sinners, with what trinkets do you commence thy spiritual trial? HOW ABOUT A TOASTER AND STYLISH LUGGAGE?!? HOW ABOUT A NEW CAR?!? Given the choice, we would humbly accept the forty days, knowing all drawn contracts eventually close, but though we have since suspected the game is rigged,

155

we nevertheless abide by your vagaries in patience and in love. So restore to us faith in our provider, here packed row-by-row under insufferable studio lights. Make known your presence to ward ill thoughts against the sinner who risks a single dollar above the highest bid, those who try for the once-round spin, all Judases of irresolute supplication. Step down through the firmament and spread your wings over us, gracious LORD, for we really really need it. Hast thou ever seen a 1994 Ford Escort? Hast thou had no choice but to pet heavily in the backseat of said chariot, making it no farther than second base? Hast thou filtered coffee through single-ply toilet paper? That is exactly what we, your faithful servants, thought. Whilst we know you created us in your image, were you to take a walk in our shoes now, our shoes which you also created as you created all things, LORD, would ye not find a hitch in thy divine stride, proclaiming, "Wow, what are these pieces of crap made out of, some sort of unrefined plastic? Plus the front's coming off, making some lame impromptu sandals." Our constant companions such as these, may they be offered up to you who can bear the weight. By your redeeming spirit, help us so that we, elbow deep in provisions necessary for a less common life, a fair portion of riches pursuant to state and federal codes, can help ourselves. Through Jesus Christ our LORD, invoking nicely? We are here, assembled in praise, cameras rolling, with nowhere else to turn. Creator of all, come on down.

For Glampers

To the great creator of this land and all the splendor I see before me: great job. It's stunning. Only a few hundred miles outside Brooklyn—thank God Simon has a car—and it's like we're somewhere completely different. Just put down your iPhone for a second and look around. This is what they mean by "majestic." That tree over there—the tall one, beyond that stumpy crooked one that only a Lorax could love—that's why people fought so many wars over this land. That tree is literally the embodiment of "purple mountain's majesty." This park is anthemic, motherfucker. And we're in it. Also, I got dibs on 'Gramming that tree later.

The air here, it feels so blessed. And same for the stars and the animals and everything else. Except for the poison ivy, which is all over the place. Carter shared a pneumonic to keep us safe: "Leaves of three? Rub it on Steve." But doesn't every plant have at least three leaves? If it doesn't it's probably dead. Anyway, it's that kind of danger that makes you feel so alive. The park ranger at the check-in—best job ever, I bet his Instagram rocks—told Marcus that more bears live in these hills than people. Which is nuts because bears are definitely endangered.

If I was a bear, I'd live here. It's probably better than Iceland or Canada or wherever other bears eke out their meager ursine existence. This park is practically made from bear food. For instance, Wendy said she saw a wild fish just sitting there in the creek—and what a perfect word for that old little river, just creaking away. If we run out of lox, I'm going to eat that fish bear-style.

Being here changes you, and I'm grateful for that. It's a chance to appreciate life and all the little things you didn't even know existed. Like those little flowers that Carmen found that didn't smell like flowers or anything at all. What's the point of flowers that don't smell? God, nature is just so fucking zen.

Matthew said when we pulled up to our campsite it was like that scene in *Contact* when Jodi Foster is in her space-time machine, looking at the swirling universe, and she starts crying and says it's so beautiful that they should've sent a poet instead (I mean, sure, or probably an astronaut). Matthew was right. It's so beautiful here it makes me feel like Jodi Foster.

Camping is like being inside a poem. Camping is like spending a weekend inside Walt Whitman's beard. I feel like I could poem about these wilds—or maybe I'll just Vine the living hell out of that songbird. But you don't have to channel Kerouac to appreciate this life. The point is to be here, to be present, and just simply experience shit. It's about reflection and observation and not thinking about the outside world. I mean, I could totally see myself just renting a tree house and summering out here. I'd tell everyone back home that they can find me just bearing it up, living life in a raccoon hat. I'll be in the land, a part of nature like moss or mountain dew. And they can come visit me anytime right here or at likeabearinthewoods.tumblr.com.

For Those Who Do Not Want To Get Angry At Their Very Nice Boyfriends

Oh Merciful God. Lend us your mercy for we are running low. We realize our boyfriends mean no harm, that they are good boyfriends. LORD, help us realize this more sincerely. Though our boyfriends have texted us that they would meet us at our apartment around seven, we take strength in remembering that boyfriends sometimes run late, forget their phone and must retrieve it, for instance, or see a godly neighbor in the street they know and get into a long conversation and then sometimes run into yet another neighbor—what are the chances?—what are the chances indeed, Oh LORD of Infinite Forgiveness. Help us to react with understanding and compassion, O God, for it is nearly half past eight, Almighty Father, half past eight. Help us remember our boyfriends are nice boyfriends, dear LORD, now and forever. *Amen*.

For Actors in Pornographic Films

Almighty God, in your infinite wisdom you have outfitted us with the necessary physical accouterments for reproduction, the stimulation and appreciation of which not only brings us great pleasure, but allows the codes of our DNA to mingle with our lovers' and produce offspring. We acknowledge our bodies as temples, as sanctuaries that are inhabitable by your Spirit, and though some of these bodies might appear to our human eyes as more inhabitable than others, we acknowledge too that we should not presume to know what physical forms you may or may not be inhabiting, or if you are, as Author of life, inhabiting, to some extent, each and every one, though at any rate it must follow that if bodies are temples then they are, as such, sacred spaces, and that two bodies coupling could therefore be seen to be two fleshy temples coming together to become one even greater temple of flesh. This intercourse, we know, is a holy thing, and should, we have been told, be entered into only by a husband and wife. But many of us have frequently if not unabashedly merged our temples with others' outside the bonds of marriage, and we have called it good, and sometimes *very* good, and we thought that perhaps you understood, that our situation, being what it was, might count as an exception, and others of us thought, like Eve considering the apple, that one time couldn't hurt, and others of us experienced great shame, and still others experienced no shame at all. We acknowledge that this is a sensitive issue, LORD, that what may seem right for some may not seem right to others, and so it's difficult, if not impossible, for us all to come to agreement about what, exactly, it's okay to do with one's body and a consenting other's. We remember King David standing upon a Jerusalem rooftop and watching a woman on another rooftop as she disrobed and slid into a tub to bathe herself, and we also remember that King David ordered this woman's poor husband to be killed in battle so he could take her as his own, and we also remember the hundreds of wives and concubines of King Solomon, whose insatiable appetite for women we would certainly not endorse today, regardless of how many wisdom-nuggets or life-lessons he happened to produce. We like to think of ourselves, LORD, as people who do more or less the right things. We like to believe we are, for the most part, civilized. For the most part, we do not take our clothes off in public, LORD. Nor do we film ourselves engaging in intercourse with our partners, except maybe for that one time, but then we quickly erased it afterwards, for fear it would fall into the hands of someone not us, and we definitely did not post it to the internet for whoever in the world might be interested to download, and so we must admit, LORD, that we find it hard to understand why actors in pornographic films do what they do, these sculpted and augmented folk who give the appearance of delighting in all manner of sexual deviances, who are fearless to the point of making us afraid—or, barring that, fearfully aroused. We who are not You and thus know not the hearts of these actors have, we admit, looked down upon them, have called them sick and perverted and sleazy, or hot, or skanky, or skanky-hot, and have, in an attempt to figure out their motives, assumed that perhaps they were simply power-hungry exhibitionists, or that they were downright too stupid to do anything else but mindlessly copulate under the hot, hot lights of a frigid studio space designed to resemble a generic apartment in Southern California, but we have also, in our more tender moments, sympathized with them, thinking "poor things" and assuming that their willingness to be tied up and tied down and spanked and sprayed with bodily fluids was a manifestation of some heretofore undiagnosed psychological trauma, inflicted upon them at some tender and therefore impressionable age, and that they do what they do because their fathers and mothers didn't love them, or loved them in all the wrong ways. We acknowledge that these assumptions are most likely irresponsible, if not ultimately patronizing, and that we are in no place to judge anyone but ourselves, and that before we attempt to remove the speck of sawdust in the eyes of our brothers and sisters, we should remove the planks in our own. Remind us, when we find ourselves tempted to think of ourselves as superior, or when we are confronted with representations of actors in pornographic films, that whatever they may be and that whatever they may do is, ultimately, none of our business. May we remember Christ, who supped with prostitutes, who shared bread with the dregs of society—not that these actors should be thought of as "dregs," only that we recognize that, historically, they have been interpreted by mainstream culture as "unorthodox" at best, and "depraved" at worst—and should we have occasion to find ourselves in their company, let us not look upon them with pity or disdain, and if we must enter into private speculations, let us wonder what they—who, though they are not us, are certainly no less human than we—may have to teach us about ourselves.

For Mild Paranoia

LORD, not just for those with tin foil hats, those grandfathers and mothers of the cause, but for our common brothers and sisters with common internet fears, we pray. For they too have hearts floating in right intention. For those who guard their children against vaccinations, we pray. For those who shout conspiracy at climate science, dear LORD. For, though they are not the ascetics who bemoan government controlled weather, though they do not have bomb cellars stocked with canned beans from Y2K, aren't their facebook posts a kind of prayer? Aren't their shared graphics with partially true statistics a kind of blind faith? LORD, You did not command us to be skeptics, but to serve with a faith we cannot prove. It has been centuries since You've visited, but You always leave signs. And when we find our phones tapped, our peanut butter recalled, our rivers cancered, and our very Cheetos engineered for addictiveness, can we not look to our mildly paranoid brothers and sisters and proclaim, "Blessed be"? For if they are not your messengers, then they are your sign of something bigger, something unseen. If we do not find the answer, oh LORD, we find ourselves again in the ineffable. And for Your glorious mysteries, let us pray.

For Those Who Perpetrated the Moon Landing Hoax

LORD Christ, when you returned to us, you commanded Thomas, "Put thy finger here, and see mine hands, and put forth thine hand, and put it into my side, and be not faithless, but faithful": Grant them the power to see who, like Thomas, walk the earth with eyes open but even so do not see, and grant us also the strength of your clear-eyed vision, so that we may keep your faith even in the face of those who would deceive us. We ask you, LORD, to have mercy upon those men who, instead of wounds or wisdom, carried back from their dusty place only more dust: photographs of Nevada and chips from the Sands and traces of showgirls' lipstick on the collar of their jumpsuits. We ask you to have mercy upon the set designers who shaped the sand and the special effects people who made the astronauts seem to float. We ask you to have mercy upon the men in the jumpsuits, the men behind the cameras, and the men behind the networks who broadcast what came out of those cameras. Have mercy upon Neil Armstrong, Michael Collins, and Buzz Aldrin. Have mercy upon Stanley Kubrick, Walt Disney, and Arthur C. Clarke. Have mercy upon John F. Kennedy, Lyndon B. Johnson, and Richard M. Nixon. Have mercy also upon those looking on who, with tongues split by the serpent, have twisted your counsel "Blessed are they who have not seen, and have believed" into "Damned are they who have seen, and have not believed." Have mercy upon him who would say: You have seen it! How can you doubt what you have seen? for he knows not that one can have faith in the LORD but one may not have faith in others before the LORD. Grant these idolaters [especially _____] the strength to roll away the moon rock holding them in their tombs of ignorance and let the direct light of your love shine upon them. Grant them your piercing gaze so that they too might see that what we have beheld so far is only through a glass screen darkly, a heavenly scene that is only a scene, not at all heavenly. LORD, we humbly ask, when you once again return to the earth, will you bring with you some of the light that lights the heavens? Not films or broadcasts but light, proof of the next world—not moon rock but moon. Will you do this so that we may finally put our fingers there? Will you do this too so that we may put our hands there, where only one man, Thomas, has ever put his hands? Will you do this so that we may finally erase this doubt? These men scaling the heights have reached out their hands, LORD. They claim they have put their hands into your side. They claim the faith you have commanded us all to have and in turn ask it of us, but we cannot have that faith in them. How shall we go on, LORD? Will you bring us a sign, another bloodied wound? Will you again suffer for our sins? Or must we suffice with these pictures of Nevada at night, of men in visors and American flags and steps for man? Will you tell us? Will you give us a sign? All of this we ask in your holy Name. *Amen.*

For Alien Abductees

LORD, we lift up those here among us whose unassuming houses in unassuming neighborhoods rattle softly – the gentle tapping of dishes in cupboards, framed photos falling from the dresser, the books shaking off the shelves – before blinding white energy pours through the windows, down the hallway, and under the threshold of their bedroom door. Be with them, LORD, as they fall frightened from their beds in their gasp for air and consciousness. Keep them safe as they float upwards towards the giant metal whale exhaling like air brakes on a big rig. And comfort them, LORD, when they wake naked, cold, and directionless in a cornfield at dawn.

We remember the few here who, while mousing for trout, find themselves in extreme foreign stillness. The river, every cedar lining the cut bank, the bottle of Fireball, all devoid of energy and motionless like some industrial biology paused the woods. And then a beam of light breaks the suspension, birds scream, fish rise violently, some flash of an operating room. Bless them when they return to their truck beds, their waders bone dry, their skin sagging, their eyebrows shaved off. Remind them not to tell their loved ones, lest they be forbidden to fish again.

Prepare the abductees to face public ridicule, shaming, and disbelief. Keep them from drinking mightily. Assure them probing does not have to be all that bad. Shelter those standing slack jawed in awe watching celestial lights hanging in the sky. Quiet the everlasting doubts. You are King of Questions. You are the Ultimate Believer.

For Guns

LORD, you have granted humanity the ingenuity to create and develop a wealth of machinery, a proliferation of devices that serve to bring us light and heat and soft places to recline and screens upon which we might view various narrative forms, so that we might be entertained and informed about the goings-on of our day, and rockets that have propelled us from our island Earth to the nearest heavenly body, and machinery to clean our utensils and cool or heat our food. Among these contrivances, LORD, for which we are most grateful, we are inclined to include our various forms of weaponry, which we have used to arm ourselves in the hunting of game and the protection of our citizenry. We have carried gun-shaped sticks as children, treasured toy pistols that popped off harmless shots. We shot movies with our parents' camcorders while holding real, though unloaded, firearms. We watched films of squinty-eyed, barrel-chested men, bald men with five o'clock shadows, men bleeding from crawling through offices whose windows had been shattered and rained shards and diamonds of glass onto the carpet and we hooted and hollered as these men blasted holes into the heads of other men. We controlled Gatlin-gun toting avatars as they worked their ways through labyrinthine passageways in Nazi castles, achieved maniacal highs from the digital blood-mist produced from blowing away our malevolent enemies. We watched that old movie with Gary Cooper who plays a kid from Tennessee who finds religion and who, despite the fact that he's the best shot with a rifle in his county and always wins the turkey shoot, becomes a conscientious objector when he's drafted into World War I, but who, sitting in a foxhole, sees his buddies dropping all around him and takes it upon himself to start picking off shooters in a German machine gun nest, and when a Major asks him, at the end of the film, why he did it, York slash Cooper says, "I done it to stop all that killing," and when we heard this, we nodded *yes*, and we thought, *of course, this is a good thing, sometimes you have to kill to stop the killing,* even if such thoughts represent a sort of circular argument and thus a conundrum of sorts, but not one, ultimately, that we felt we failed to understand. We have held guns—the guns of our friends, the guns of our fathers and grandfathers—in our hands and felt a charge—a very large charge—as we turned them sideways slash gangster-style and pursed our lips and fired imaginary bullets at imaginary bad guys. And so, even though we don't own guns—or maybe we do—we do our best to try to understand why people do. But when the gun people come to our town—a town that has seen its share of bloodshed, a town in which a mass shooting occurred not so long ago, during which a mentally unstable kid, a child himself, really, entered the classrooms of our university, and, armed with guns and carrying rounds upon rounds of ammunition, began firing bullets into the bodies of our students, some of whom jumped through windows to escape while others played dead and while still others bled to death on the floor—and when the gun people show up at a booth they've paid for at our summer festival, and when they hand out free orange stickers that say, "Guns Save Lives," let us not, LORD, go mad. Let us not yell at them. Let us not engage. Let us not point out the logical impossibility that a machine whose primary purpose is to kill can save lives. Let us not assume that a person who would wear a "Guns Save Lives" sticker on their camouflage shirt is a verifiable moron and possibly a danger to society. Let our hearts not be troubled when we imagine pork-faced juggernauts casually toting AK-47s around their backyards, but let us pray for all those who have known the blistering sting of firearms: the desert soldier dragging half a leg to a ditch, the seven-year-old whose last sight is the spaghetti noodle stuck to the ceiling of a cafeteria where a masked shooter unleashed a storm of bullets, an elderly woman whose brains were scattered in a yard in exchange for her purse. Let us honor their lives by metastasizing and thus rerouting our anger. Let us pray—futile as it may be—that all of our gun-toting citizens find comfort. And, therefore, peace.

An Exhortation: Against Dread

For Administration of a Holy Sacrament
Eximius Litania

To be sung.

Officiant:

All of us Afraid on Earth: that coming long night of death will fall like a curtain sure as the morning sun is born. But for as long as we've been afraid and painted pictures, human dread has had an earthly home. For it is within the holy mystery of imagination that we are all made one with heaven, and hell, with life, and death, all of us a body, how many billion members of this round, and quaking, striving thing alive, which sort of explains, for the most part, anyway, why so many of us enjoy horror movies.

Because, have in mind, death awaits like those murderously cruel and patient boys in Michael Haneke's Austrian modern horror classic Funny Games, which is to say death awaits outside our homes, will invite itself inside, invade at its discretion, and once within our boundaries will hurt and play and torture and take from the living when it wants; and pray let us recall that said film actually plays with the audience, that both boys look at the camera, look at us, and they smirk—they wink!— that they use a remote control within the film to rewind the very film we are watching and deny us any chance for redemption, and, well, it's infuriating, yes, but also uncannily comforting because we like to think death has a face, eyes, and a mouth, hands, and fingers for strangling and for cutting, and this verily scares the shit out of us, literally. Not the "shit" part, necessarily, unless of course that has happened to some, which it probably has, and if so, we are not judging (lest we be judged), but literally with regard to the "out" part: it takes the scare out of us and casts it somewhere else, away from the body, and gives it a home in the air of this world, so as to not let the dread of death build in our blood like a poison until our nightmares spill over into day and we soon convince ourselves that if the world is out to kill us then by some corrupted grace it is better we strike first and hurt.

For if we are to share rightly in the celebration of the holy mystery, in the uncountable acts of our imagination, and be nourished by its sustenance, we must remember the dignity of this holy sacrament: be not dreadful, and let us not forget that evil itself is an act of transcendence, albeit a perverted one, as it allows us to leave this dying body and inflict that dying on another; and let us also not forget there's more than one kind of transcendence, there's the "evil" thing, yes, like we just mentioned, and religion, of course, but there's other stuff like really good booze, or first-time-in-a-long-time sex, or Eclipse Enterprise's *True Crime Trading Cards, Series Four: Serial Killers and Mass Murderers*. One must consider at least two major things about such a collection. One: why is such a thing so attractive to children? To adults? To collectors? Why, pray tell, o All-Knowing One, do we fetishize evil and its doers? And also why does such a thing go for only twenty dollars on ebay, when some of us paid nearly that much when they first came out back in 1992? More to the point, why do some of us keep such a terrible thing, in the first place, no matter how many times we move, now matter where we go, from Atlanta, to California, to New York, uselessly taking up junk drawer-space and shelf-space, the cards not even boxed anymore, but instead sitting in loose piles, in a clear plastic bag, the painted faces of each killer on every card like so many heads asphyxiating all at once. Two: We also now realize that the stats and facts on these very cards are no longer even close to sufficient as there have been two decades of malfeasant vicissitudes inflicted upon this world since initial publication, which brings us back to the starting point.

Declare:

Officiant and Congregation, now standing: O let us make something of our dread.

Congregation: Card number 184, Dorothy Puente.

Officiant: She who by fifty-nine years of age had killed and disappeared twenty-five boarders from her state-licensed senior citizen housing facility in Sacramento in order to access their social security incomes, thereby increasing her own, and as much as the Social Security Act was an attempt to limit what were seen as the dangers of modern American elder life, Dorothy Puente attempted to limit those same dangers for herself by inflicting mortal dangers on the innocence of others.

Congregation: Card number 171, Carl Panzram.

Officiant: He who confessed to killing at least twenty-two men and raping and assaulting more than one thousand, not because he was homosexual, as his memoirs specifically point out, but because he wanted to humiliate and dominate, yes, he who was hung from the gallows of Leavenworth and said even unto his hangman, "I wish the entire human race had one neck, and I had my hands around it."

Congregation: Card number 192, Laurie Wasserman Dann.

Officiant: She who one dreadful morning filled her car with three handguns, at least one bomb, and several bags of poisoned treats for children—rice krispie squares, popcorn, and juice sippy-packets—and left them at the homes of locals she was sure had meant her harm, she who attempted bombing one school and entered yet another firing bullets, killing one small boy—let us learn and remember his name—and next confined by gunpoint a family in the basement of their home, and afterward set that home on fire, yes, she who despite flailing efforts to ward off harm, shot herself dead before inflicting more mortal acts on this earth.

Congregation: Card number 183, Gary Stephen Krist.

Officiant: He who confessed to three murders, and to the kidnapping of a twenty-year-old young woman and the subsequent act of burying her alive, in a box, for three and half days, from which she rose alive—

Congregation: —as if Christ from Hades, because Gary Stephen Krist's attempt to inflict his mortality on another and bury it in earth did not avail.

Officiant and Congregation: If we engage the sacrament, and understand evil as a thing made manifest, a thing not alive—

Officiant: —and choose to watch, say, really graphic horror movies, or maybe even hold onto certain things others might find disturbing, and perhaps go so far as to hide them when our in-laws come over, even if we cannot exactly articulate *why* we keep some things so ugly and useless, things so representative of all things deathly, in trading card format, to boot (perhaps we can think of such stuff as a talisman, this clear plastic bag overfilled with 110 faces of death, reminding us that they are all but fearsome exaggerations of our possible selves), then we will live each day amidst both life and death, amongst all sorts of heavens and all sorts of hells; and though we, too, eventually go join our long gone children and so lovely wife, all three lost forever in a single random act of human violence, we will know such is life, like it or not. Amen.

For Video Game Characters Who Are Running Out of Hit Points Right in the Middle of the Last Boss Fight

Holy Trinity, one God,
Have mercy on your humble servants who are just trying to defeat this last boss.

From all evil, from all new attacks, from all glitches and freezes,
Good LORD, deliver us.

With special attacks undiscovered, with super weapons yet unused, with potions yet undrunk,
Good LORD, deliver us.

By your glorious Resurrection and Ascension, may we similarly be resurrected, may we complete this game, may we not perish in this very last fight after many days and weeks and months of constant battle,
Good LORD, deliver us.

We sinners beseech you to hear us, LORD Christ: Cannot you see that even now this is turning red and flashing? That even now he is temporarily weakened and we could totally finish him if we just had more HP? Dear LORD, may it please you to deliver the soul of your servant from the power of this boss and from eternal video game death,
We beseech you to hear us, good LORD.

Jesus, bearer of our items:
Have mercy on us.

Jesus, bearer of the world map and compass:
Lend us your strength and then roll the final cut scene.

For the Unlikely Heroes of Apocalypse Movies

Thank you, LORD, for the beginning of every global ending: toilet water flushing counterclockwise in the northern hemisphere, too much lightning or not enough wind, tsunamis littering beaches with the old plastic of dead jellyfish, birds flying rabid into European plazas, wolves dying of inexplicable disease above the permafrost. Thank you, LORD, for the wolves and for their dying, because how else would our lowly lupine expert become The Only Man Who Can Possibly Save The World? We need to see him, every him—the humble analyzer of DNA, the quiet arbolist, the loneliest ornithologist, the crypto-meteorologist in bifocals—we need to see each man close his laptop and take a bullet or an asteroid to the chest. Let him turn away from his swivel chair, throw off his lab coat, clutch his sheath of charts and surge forth into the gloaming. Let him sound the alarm. Let him rise into his mythos. Let him claim the junior high school that will someday bear his name.

And thank you, LORD, for our crypto-meteorologist's estranged wife and our lupine expert's disabled son, because they will make our heroes men again. Let them be trapped by terrorists, buried by too much snowfall over the shelled ruins of iconic skyscrapers—let their peril drive our heroes onto snowplows, or speedboats, so they can ride over the frosted or flooded Eastern Seaboard while their sidekicks seduce the beautiful daughters of third-world presidents. Thank you for these fools' errands, LORD. We would feel nothing without them. And thank you for the inscrutable and gratuitous technology that makes them possible: for screens that are played like pianos and keyboards that glow in the dark of the night, for computers that hold crawl spaces like circuit-studded stomachs—thank you for these spaces in which our crypto-meteorologist DOES THE RIGHT THING and TYPES THE RIGHT CODE or maybe punches a shark in the face, if he has to, if a limb has been lost.

Thank you for the end of every world, LORD. May no ending happen too quickly. May the major cities of the world fall like dominoes in slow-mo: give us the leaning tower finally crashing into Pisa; give us Big Ben exploded and Cairo on fire; give us Tokyo businessmen fighting dolphins in the street. Give Manhattan to heaven and Los Angeles to hell. Give our meteorologist and his marriage a second chance in all the wreckage; give him a love that can withstand statistically impossible tsunamis and jellyfish strewn upon the sand like scarves and armies of brown birds flying straight from the white hot eye of the sun. Let his sidekick fuck that dictator's girl at least once before the second meteor hits. Let their progeny start the colony on Mars.

But dear LORD—in the end, at the last—please let the second meteor hit. Don't deny anyone his junior high school. Give our secondary heroes their embryonic Eves and Adams. Let everyone fall into the asteroid chasm. Let everyone blister in the too-close sun. Let everyone perish. Let no one live.

For My Neighbor's Quick, Painless Death

Dear God,

Do You know who's a real asshole? And I know You do know, but I'm just going to say it anyway. My neighbor, Chuck Jensen, that's who. His friend Kristy's okay, I guess, though when I first saw her on the pool deck, I had no idea she was Chuck's paramour. This was before the lawn signs, before I knew Marilyn was gone for good. I'd just seen her with their youngest—Munson? Bunson?—packing the car for college. A few days later, I'm up in my study, sweating over my résumé, when I see this lovely girl laid out by their pool. I thought she was Bunson's friend, then remembered Bunson didn't live there anymore. Whoever she was, she was ruining my day, laughing and screaming into her phone, all oiled up under my window. I smoked a joint and thought about making dinner so Sylvia wouldn't have to cook. Maybe I'd apply to culinary school. Maybe I'd become a badass chef, tattooed and furious. I even started walking toward the kitchen, but that's when I noticed the lawn sign, "God Has Given Us a Christian Nation." I got stuck for a second, wondering if England had been right way back when, if the pilgrims were just a bunch of assholes who deserved to be persecuted and shipped away, not at all the beloved, buckle-shoed heroes of Thanksgiving. I got so lost in my musing, I forgot to make dinner, and Sylvia ended up cooking again, something bland and nearly inedible.

Kristy disappeared for a few days after that, but once the weather cleared, she returned to the pool deck, topless. I'd had a good run, had almost finished a draft of the résumé, but now my workday was ruined. A new sign had sprouted on the Jensen's lawn that morning: "At Least the War on Healthcare's Going Well," and I wondered if it was the topless girl's work, if she was rebutting Chuck's puritanical idiocy with her own slogan. I walked across the lawn and rang the bell, praying Marilyn

176

wouldn't answer, but it was Kristy who opened the door, bright and cheerful in a white robe over her bikini. I introduced myself as the next door neighbor, the carriage house neighbor.

"Chuck's tenant?" she said, and I said, "Right next door," and we chatted for a minute—about climate change, I recall—and she smiled, vaguely, waiting, until I asked if she was Bunson's friend, and she said, "Bunson's down in Nashville now, at Vanderbilt," and I was like, "Oh, that's right. Marilyn—Mrs. Jensen—drove her down last week. Are you staying with the Jensens?"

That's when she told me Marilyn was "gone" and that she—Kristy—was Chuck's friend—Mr. Jensen, she called him, a nice, if horrifying, touch.

"The sign out front," I said. "Did you put it there?"

"The new one?" she said. "About the war on healthcare?"

"It's brilliant," I said, and she said, "Yeah, I know. We've been getting into all kinds of shit, Mr. Jensen and me—capital markets and arbitrage, government regulation and the church. All the deep institutional forces. All the major levers. The fed. The Jews. International banking. The Freemasons."

"The Jews?" I said. "Really? The Freemasons?"

"You might not realize this," she said, "but the Jews are the original Christians, which is why we have to work so hard for a Palestinian homeland, even while developing settlements. Empathy's critical here. Love machines are what we need, Chuck says," and I thought, of course Chuck says that, and Kristy said, "There's only one right side in any interaction—the loving side," and I had to get away from her, but when I told Sylvia about it that night, she said she didn't want to talk about Chuck and Kristy anymore, ever, and we went to sleep angry again.

The next morning a new sign appeared: "Religion Is What Keeps the Poor From Murdering the Rich—Napoleon." I saw it driving back from Stan's house, where I get my weed, but I couldn't tell what it meant. Chuck's the one with Jesus fish on his cars. Was he misunderstanding Napoleon's words, or was he rich and religious and glad of it, because religion kept poor people like me from murdering rich people like him? I didn't even have religion yet. And I've never tried to kill him. Was he merely affiliating himself with Napoleon? I walked the weed to my study, Kristy below wearing nothing now, tanning and tanning, though she was already perfectly tan. I couldn't see a single tan line on her, even through my binoculars.

Days passed with no progress on my résumé, no new messages on Chuck's lawn, until this morning, when these words appeared: "Restore America's Decency Laws!" I rolled a joint and smoked it while Kristy tanned, the sound of her braying laughter washing over me like warm summer rain. Then Chuck walked onto the deck, a horrible first. Kristy was there, nude, and I was in my study, keeping track of everything—it's not even noon yet—and Chuck started kissing her, deeply, then stripped and lay beside her, totally naked, and I was like, they're gonna mate down there, please, no, they're gonna mate right in front of me, but they didn't mate, and I looked through my binoculars at the tattoos on Chuck's pecs, one of Shakespeare, winking and throwing gang signs, the other a balloon headed Rush Limbaugh, a giant cigar coming out of his face. I ran downstairs and outside. There was a Prius in Chuck's driveway, with two bumper stickers: "Liberal Judges are Destroying America," and, "Wage Peace!"

LORD, I have prided myself on my principals of tolerance. I practice the peace I'd teach if I were a teacher. I've never once acted out of white male entitlement, nor earned more than Sylvia—for equal work or otherwise. But I wanted to key that Prius in the worst way. I ran upstairs to roll another joint, but Chuck and Kristy were still below, still not mating, thank God, thank You, but holding hands so sweetly between their lawn chairs it was all I could do to keep from shouting something awful at them. Sylvia says I've become obsessive, and maybe I have. She also says I have two weeks to find a job, any job, or she's walking away from everything we've built together.

But how am I supposed to focus on my résumé when I've got Kristy naked out back and Chuck beside her and all these signs and slogans I can't interpret? I fell to my knees beside my window. Chuck noticed me looking down at them through my binoculars. He waved, winking, then flipped me off, before turning his finger around and flashing a peace sign, his expression so gentle, so kind, so *lamb*like, I wished one of us would be struck dead then and there.

And I *was* struck—not dead, but struck nonetheless. On my knees at my window, I realized I was praying—*am* praying—something I've never done in my life.

Praying for You to annihilate Chuck on his pool deck naked.

And still he smiles at me like a lamb!

I know he's more evolved than I am, LORD, a better man. But I can't bear to live beside him anymore, not like this, with Kristy oiled up all over the place, waiting to mate, and Sylvia making plans to leave me. I'd pray to be a better man if I thought it would do any good, or maybe that's what I am praying for—to be a better man, to see Chuck's death as tragic, not just for the world, but for me, to stop coveting Kristy, to learn to love, to learn compassion, to learn to mourn something other than myself, to beg You, LORD, for his quick, painless passing. Even if I can't be a better man, I want to believe I can, and that must be worth something. Please make me a better man, LORD, capable of mourning. Please be gentle with me, with Chuck. Please be gentle with us all.

179

A Prayer Cycle to be Uttered by Five Enemies

(recite simultaneously, daily for five days, or until desired results are obtained)

[1.]
Monday: LORD, my enemies beset me. They surround me like hair.
　　　Please help them find a way to give me a break
　　　so I can stop wanting to murder them.

Tuesday: LORD, my enemies are at my throat. I think they also ate
　　　all the granola. Please help me resist the urge to fashion a crude,
　　　passive-aggressive sign to dissuade them.

Wednesday: LORD, help me with my murderous thoughts. They beset me
　　　like enemies, which is a pickle since my enemies are also
　　　their object. I think you get the idea.

Thursday: LORD, seriously. I forgot to brush my teeth this morning.
　　　I don't think I have to tell you I'm getting burned out here.
　　　It's my enemies and my hating them.

Friday: LORD, I'm taking a half-day.

[2.]
Monday: LORD, my enemies continue to beset me. There is so much hair,
　　　I'm not even sure what I'm looking at.
　　　I live in a drain.

Tuesday: I dunno, LORD, I haven't seen my enemies. I think they might
　　　be on vacation. They probably should have informed me,
　　　but I'm kind of glad they didn't.

Wednesday: LORD, who is the true enemy here, anyway? If I can't
　　　rust myself, I find it hard to trust you. Please help me
　　　not think about this.

Thursday: LORD, I distinctly heard one of my enemies whisper
　　　something under his breath about the beard I'm growing.
　　　Should I just shave it off?

Friday: LORD, I'm have a meeting off-site this morning, so I may
  not come in until after lunch. I'll let my enemies know.

[3.]

Monday: Besetting me, LORD. I know, it almost sounds like they are
  doing me a service, but language is weird and sinful.
  My enemies disturb my lunch hour. They interrupt me
  as I try to do math!

Tuesday: I'm exceedingly sleepy, LORD, but I did see my enemies on the bus
  this morning, and it didn't escape my notice that they were
  reading something trashy.

Wednesday: Ugh. LORD, please let there be ibuprofen in the break room. Also,
  let there be enough for my enemies.

Thursday: Every time I catch a glimpse of myself reflected, LORD, I think
  of my enemies. I know I should exercise more regularly.

Friday: OUT OF COFFEE?!?!

[4.]

Michael Robartes: What my enemies fail to understand — among other things,
LORD
  — are the fundamental contradictions that ground our very existence. I don'
  have to tell you, I know, that everything that exists and acts exists and acts
  only by virtue of a contrary, a shadow. But my enemies, they aren't getting it

Tuesday: I'm the day after the first day of the week, which makes me its dumb kid
  brother. I have the highest statistical probability of being smothered with a
  pillow. LORD, can you help?

Wednesday: Oh, this coffee tastes good with a little bit of fat. It doesn't matter wha
  kind: milk fat, nut fat, whatever. Thank you for this synergy, LORD. May it
  betoken greater synergy with my enemies and their silo-breaking collocation

The Dancer: FAME! I'm gonna live forever. Make you remember by name!

Friday: If I were going to work a nap in here at lunch, that would be cool, right?

I mean it's my time.

[5.]

Monday: I had a dream, LORD, wherein you and I stood together on a hill of
    my enemies' hair. It was sort of like a never-before-seen deleted scene
    from *Eraserhead* or maybe *Clerks*. Anyway, you were you, but you didn't
    look like you. But I knew it was you. The hair looked just like my
    enemies' hair.

Jason Robards: My sad eyes, LORD! How they cast an air of grave
    sobriety over the break room.

Wednesday: Always the odd one out! Dialectics are divisible by two,
    LORD. My enemies treat me like a rump. But in my relative muteness,
    I am one to their collective clamor. Let them consider my absence.
    How would they walk?

Thursday: I drive a Prius. I'm optimistic. All things must pass, but this too
    shall pass.

Cher: DOYOUBELIEVEINALIFEAFTALOVE???

[Alternate verse]

Monday: I'm stuck on hold, LORD, with one of my enemies.
    Why must there be music?
    Would that there were only silence.

Tuesday: One of my enemies, well... ok it was me, told me
    that his Dad said you
    might not exist, LORD.

William Butler Yeats: Yesterday when I saw the dry and leafless vineyards at
    the very edge of the motionless sea, or lifting their brown stems from
    almost inaccessible patches of earth high up on the cliff-side, or met at
    the turn of the path the orange and lemon trees in full fruit, or blue
    and blue, I murmured, as I have countless times, 'I have been part of it
    always and there is no escape, forgetting and returning life after life like
    an insect in the roots of the grass.' But murmured it without terror, in

exultation almost.

Thursday: I'm taking a long weekend. It's Friday, bitches!!!

Friday: I shower in the morning and also again at night. I try
to keep the residues of my enemies from one world protected
from the noses of my enemies in the next.

For Signs

LORD, cradle this
snowbank and me:

it does not care
what I think of it

and I do not care
what it thinks

of me. We share this
kind of *port de bras*.

For now is the winter
of my deep regret,

and objects seem
closer than they appear.

Seven states away
from home, I write

about torture and lie
awake in a residential

hotel with a mauve-
and-tan kitchenette,

and though I surely
should have seen it

coming (my sleepless
nights, his frequent

departures to Seattle), my
husband divorces me over

the phone. LORD,
I know you

are not responsible
for damage or theft. Please:

pick up after
your dog. No matter

what the fluttering
blue plastic

bag under
that language means,

move over
bacon because I

have a plane to
catch and I want to enter

the airport of my failure
with grace. Two

bags checked and a whiskey
before takeoff. A swift

ascent and no
smoking or planes

falling out of the sky.

Let the cartoon

buttons ding
in agreement and the overhead

masks help
themselves before others.

Someone will
offer admonitions

about the exits
cheerfully, indistinctly.

LORD, if you see
something, say something.

For Children at Bedtime

Will you go to sleep? No, really. We have gathered here, as we usually do, around this time, hoping to send you to the land of slumber. It is our solemn duty to give you a full night's sleep, and it is your duty, as son or daughter, to submit to the darkness, not the darkness of ignorance or the darkness of waywardness but the darkness that comes when you close your eyes. Please close them. Your heart and mind and body is intended by God to rest, to recover from the tumult of the day and to grow. In this crib is the time for expansion and digestion and rest. Yours and also ours. We beseech thee, really we do. We implore thee. Wholeheartedly. To the heavens we don't beg but we would. Will you, baby, forsaking the light of day and the frolick of the sun, enter into the peace of sleep? Will you, baby, relax. Will you, while witness to the honking of the everlasting trucks outside your window, and the voices of the drunk pedestrians, and the barking of the of dogs, give yourself to union with almighty unconsciousness? Praise be yours if you will. Amen.

A Thanksgiving for the First Full Night of Sleep after the Birth of the First Child

Or

Give Praise, For She Has Slept Through the Night!

Dear Friends: The first full night of sleep after the birth of the first child is a joyous event in the life of the family. We bid you, therefore, to (quietly, if not silently) join us in giving heart-burstingly happy thanks to Almighty God, our heavenly father, the LORD of both light and nightlight. Let's (use our inside voices to) say together:

We love the LORD because he has heard the infant's wails—every two or three hours all through the night for one hundred and eighty-six consecutive nights—and inclined his ear to sympathy.

Whenever we call upon the LORD to intervene—as in, *please merciful savior, render upon us a night of continuous sleep so that we may never again hallucinate a foaming parakeet sea beneath the baby's bed*—he hears the voice of our desperation.

Whenever we call upon the LORD to arbitrate—as in, *please merciful savior, remind our loving spouse whose turn it is to function as a living cushion and/or human swing as dawn breaks through the venetians*—he knows the truth of our resignation.

Whenever we call upon the LORD to reconcile—as in, *please merciful savior, convince our sisters-in-law that we appreciate the advice, but we've read the Ferber and the Weissbluth and the Sears*—he senses our internal assignation.

We love the LORD because he has heard the voice of our supplication. Gracious is the LORD, so full of compassion. He bore witness to the driving away from the gas pump with the cap on the roof of the car and knew that it was time. He bore witness to the dropping of the breast pump parts down the storm drain and knew that it was right. He bore witness to the fellow employees ignoring the blatant cubicle napping and knew that it was kind. Gracious is the LORD, so full of compassion. He let our little one sleep.

How shall we repay the LORD for the rest he has given us?

We will lift the sippy cup of salvation and praise his name!

We will recall the promises made in moments of extreme desperation and donate to charity!

We will carry his news forth to others of our ilk! You will sleep again, dear friends. Oh, yes, you will sleep again.

Hallelujah and Amen.

For Beds

Merciful God, we humbly thank Thee for setting the earth on its rotation around the sun, thus providing humanity with periods of light that permit us, as we go about our daily business, to recognize with relative clarity the things of the earth, and for the atmospheric changes and angles of the sun that allow us to sense the progression of time and thus acknowledge all manner of climatological differences. So too do we thank Thee for creating a period of darkness during which our eyes might find respite and our minds repose, and where we might also experience a reprieve from sense-making, most palpably experiencing, in our dream-states, the joys and terrors of embarking upon adventures much greater in scope than we would ever hope to undergo during our comparatively prudent daytime excursions. But most of all, oh LORD, we thank Thee for the beds upon which we sleep, and for which we too often take for granted, failing to remember the hay-or-leaf-stuffed animal skin mattresses of yore, or the goat-skin waterbeds of Persia, or the heaped palm-boughs of Egypt. We recognize now the discoveries of vulcanized rubber and box springs, of memory foam invented by scientists employed in our national aeronautics and space program. We are thankful too, oh Heavenly Father, for the accouterments that adorn these beds, for the linens of silk or cotton or flannel, for blankets of down, for pillows of goose-feathers or microbeads. We are thankful for box springs, oh LORD, and that our beds are raised above the ground, upon which roam the countless creatures that might do us harm, and for the space below these beds, where, as youngsters, we imagined monstrous, slobbering entities, and where now old socks and dust balls have created a netherworld of forgotten things that, when spied upon, remind us that unseen spaces exist in our homes, and that these too deserve, from time to time, our attention. We therefore ask a blessing upon these our beds, that they may not do us harm but fulfill their promise in providing us a place to safely slumber, that they might be rafts upon which we lie to escape the storms of life, and that furthermore, they may remain a place where children are forbidden to jump—if only so that children may discover the joys of benign transgressions, so long as they do not fall and crack open their heads on our dressers or nightstands—and where lonely souls recline to read or bathe in the glow of television, and where couples unite in joyful lovemaking, a space into which children crawl when awoken from night terrors, and where poor souls who have lost loved ones might curl up into the positions they first took in the wombs of their mothers and, grasping wadded tissues, dab at their weeping eyes. Forgive us LORD, if we are to forget the luxuries afforded to us of our beds, and keep us ever mindful of those who sleep tonight upon surfaces that were not made with comfort in mind, those who, for reasons that are unknown to us, face conditions we cannot and therefore do not imagine, and should these poor souls die before they wake, grant them a final dream in which they lie with their lovers on a mattress of memory foam, the pressure-sensitive polyurethane surface molding to the shapes of their bodies, so that sleepers and beds, in the end, become one.

Peace Prayer

"God turn your face to me
and grant me peace"—Internet prayer

To cocoon oneself in God as if submerged
in a river seems an easier kind of peace; what God

can you stare at and be peaceful? Does not his face
blind like a floodlight, burn your pupils

out to dark stars? Doesn't it become a little analogy, instead,
of bright light and moths? But what do I know

about God, my hair smelling of sulfer and unable
to fit the right words together in the right order

to win the friend back as if human interaction
were Legos or Tetris. How disappointing,

the world and those in it, particularly myself. This morning
I tried to pet my own shoulder like a cat, thinking, "poor

kitten, I'm sorry." And then laughed. There is the version
of the story where all this grief makes sense

and every lost person was beloved—the face at supermarket
turning towards you as she rummages through cans; the eternal silenc

at the other end of your g-chat. There is also the version
that it was just so much noise

and now that that's over
other noise fills the gap:

birds in their senseless chatter like broken glass
the other friends you'd forgotten

click of the streetlights changing so the cars pass.

By the Power of All that Is Seen and Unseen

In the evening we long for you. Stand toe to the edge of the tree line and think about turning back to the sun setting behind the barn. We step forward. We search for you in the cracked light between empty branches and never question that we are moving together in the same skeletal system alongside deer and salamander and spiders who graffiti the air with delicate lines of silk. All creatures here and below. We are organs. *In word or song.* Hearts drumming against the dead beat of night. We are. Begotten, not made, our soft footed monster. Our counter primal part. In the evening we long for you. Stand toe to the edge and feel we are suicidal in this graceless longing in which we live believing. To love you and to have love taken away. To still hope. Bipedal humanoid to all our blessings flow. Even if you never leave your cave, we will still search for you where the dew drops of almost shimmer soft. We will pray. In the name of our mythical thing, our Sasquatch, our fur.

Evening Prayer

Dock LORD
your boat at my door
tonight.
The pier's fringe
falls on itself
and is raised by you.
Take my badge of
disbelief,
the scab I forage in,
lift the hammered copper
from my wrists.

With your oceanic hands,
with brief green shoots
and the stubble of lighthouses
with my irrefutable body
please LORD tend
the flogging sheet
of my soul.

Dock LORD
your boat at my door tonight.
I'll be waiting
by the thick black mark
you dug into the wood.
Carry my mistakes on your
shoulders, and unbind
the parcel of my body:

Take away my sticks, stow
my tired speech,
turn me inside out
so my shiny part

faces the sky, so it can
take upon itself all the stars,
all the dumb blue oil of the night.

Four Prayers for the New Year

1.

Before the age of 13, I had my head shaved four times at various South Indian temples for religious and cultural reasons. Tonsuring in Hinduism is metaphoric, the baring of the skull meant to represent a cleansing of the soul, a total absolution and a submission to God. Therefore, Tamilian parents may subject their children to this tradition when they do particularly well on a mathematics exam or like me, have lived their entire life in a foreign country. I remember well the pujari, or priest, taking a straight razor to my skull, gently, but in sudden long strokes, as if shucking corn husks, the back of my head newly bare, tingling.

Once in Tirupathi Temple in Andhra Pradesh, under the gilt dome of the vimanam and the bejeweled eye of LORD Sri Venkateswara, my cousin and I both had our heads shaved, then massaged with cool sandalwood paste. We were carried off bald and emboldened on the shoulders of my relatives feeling like little heroes and treated accordingly by the aunties who fed us laddus for the rest of the day. Apparently Tirupathi harvests over a ton of human hair each day, raising over $6 million dollars annually for its treasuries after auctioning the shorn hair off to wig-makers. But I didn't know, nor would I have cared about that back then.

Standing in front of a mirror and pulling back my hair to inspect my slowly receding hairline with the dispassionate gaze of an environmental geologist considering the effects of coastal erosion, I pray to feel again the way I did as that young boy who had lost all his hair.

2.

How many times have I been ripped off?

Once at Action Automotive in Berlin, Connecticut, pronounced with the accent on the first syllable, so that according to urban legend, the town would not be confused with its German counterpart, where Dave the mechanic wiped his greasy hands on his coveralls and assured me that he had the perfect vehicle for me—a 1998 VW Passat, fully loaded and meticulously inspected, that he would sell to me for less than blue book. Flash forward two months: I am stranded on the side of the highway, green liquid dripping onto the asphalt, sulfuric smoke dissipating skyward. No warranty means that for only two grand, Dave would be happy to repair the transmission.

Another mechanical swindle (note to self: don't buy objects the workings of which you don't understand, at least not without an expert in tow), this time in Northern Cyprus, regarded as occupied territory by everyone save Turkey, where I am on exchange with a faculty member at Eastern Mediterranean University and living in Famagusta. Every day on my way to work I pass a storefront that has mechanical airplanes, remote control tanks and in a place of prominence in the window, a shiny chrome-blue scooter available for the equivalent of $500. The shop owner tells me that Jamal owns the bike and when he arrives, he's swarthy with tattooed biceps and a denim vest. He doesn't speak English, so the owner translates. "Jamal says he never race this bike. Keep it top quality. He after market the engine. Super-primo." Convinced, I buy the bike. Five kilometers from the shop, it sputters to a halt. I push it back to the store, sweating and panting, where Jamal is lounging out front smoking a Camel. Not only does he refuse to fix the bike, he feigns ignorance, claims never to have laid eyes on me, nor the bike. The shop owner shrugs apologetically. "Sorry Jamal always a little bit çılgın! But once you leave store, I not know what happens" (second note to self: never buy a scooter from a man named Jamal).

Years earlier at Place Pigalle, on the border between the 9th and 18th arrondissements in Paris, near the street with the Sexodrome and the Grand Guignol theatre where a Toulouse Lautrec-sized Moroccan man with a knitted coolie cap and patched corduroys sold me a baggie of subpar herbs de provence. My college friend and I smoked two and half joints before finally convincing ourselves we had been taken. I recall our trembling anticipation turning virulently to disgust and sophomoric curses. I also wonder whether that extra half joint was really necessary?

Remembering my vivid, recurrently hateful dreams of humiliating Dave, Jamal and the Moroccan dwarf, making them grovel before me, penitent and embarrassed, I pray that my spirit will release their burdens and that I can forgive them once and for all.

3.

Without desire, would I become serene, emergent, responsive to higher vibrations, able to look down at my body as an odd if miraculous quirk of muscle and bone, to mull myself from an astral plane, on the path to becoming a bodhisattva? Or would I be a pallid, languid sponge, a veritable non-entity soaking up nutrients, incapable of being swept away by any great passion or transformed into something resembling the thunderhead and the tidal wave?

What about the plethysmograph, that instrument used to measure vaginal blood-flow and lubrication, which shows that range of potential arousal is much greater in women than it is in men? What is it about pronouncing those syllables slowly—ple-thys-mo-graph—maybe even putting a suffix onto it and turning it into a condition, a mania—ple-thys-mo-graph-ia—that gets me hard? Why is it so hard for me to write 'hard'? That rereading the sentence I blush but simultaneously don't want to admit to myself that I am blushing nor that I am hard?

Then there's that silent film from the early nineteen-twenties, starring the androgynous Ivor Novello, called "The Man Without Desire" about an 18th century Venetian put into suspended animation only to reawaken in the 20th century, finding life drab and savorless. The same Ivor Novello who seduced, then just as quickly discarded the poet Siegfried Sassoon, who destroyed his diary entries from that period in response. Remembering that line from a Browning poem from the film—"What of soul was left, I wonder, when the kissing had to stop?"—I wonder how Sassoon might have responded to that question?

The problem of sex seems to be that the act of doing it can never satisfy the desire for doing it. Take the Sanskrit word tanhā, which means craving and is considered a primary cause in the arising of dukkha, or suffering. As opposed to aspiration, or monlam, a longing for something that can lead to greater mindfulness and eventual liberation from suffering. De-sire desire, I tell myself. You are not its father. It is not your child. Repeat. Rinse. Repeat. But then I see a gloved finger searching in a scalloped coin purse or the sepal-whorl of a prize-winning orchid and my mantra disperses into the moist air. I pray to be able to differentiate between healthy and unhealthy desires.

4.

This being human is a guest house.
Every morning a new arrival[1].

The new year. A time of rebirth and resolution, born out of reflection on the year that has just passed. 2013: Surveilence, twerking, health care, gun violence, hashtags, sequesters, the Pope, drones, debt; a litany for the talking heads. But sitting at my desk, wrinkling my brow in remembrance, it is the Sufi dervishes who come to mind, conjured in a chapel in Athens, Georgia by Coleman Barks who read his translations of Rumi in a Chattanooga drawl, the words spinning out from his mouth like electrons around a nucleus.

---

[1] Excerpted from "The Guest-House," by Jelaluddin Rumi, translated by Coleman Barks in *The Essential Rumi* (Harper-Collins, 2004).

A joy, a depression, a meanness,
some momentary awareness comes
as an unexpected visitor.

Whatever ills I suffered—and last year there were plenty
to choose from, from a broken finger that still hasn't straight-
ened itself out to having my laptop with a summer's worth of
writing pilfered on a Metro North train—plus whatever joys,
from being fêted by the American embassy in Singapore to seeing my daughter score her first goal in Peewee soccer, I find I
am neither the sum nor the apotheosis of those experiences,
positive or negative.

Be grateful for whatever comes.
because each has been sent
as a guide from beyond.

Could it be that everything that happened to me happened to you as well? That I am the Syrian family whose home
has been shelled to rubble and you are the unburied corpses
in the wake of Super Typhoon Haiyan. That I am the British
grandmother sentenced to death for being a drug mule in Indonesia and you are Nelson Mandela taken off his life-support
machine in South Africa. That I filter through you like water
through an aquifer, leaving us both permeable, porous, con-
glomerate and fractured, in perpetual, clamorous motion, and
yet thereby stilled into silence. That each one of us is a single
stitch in a vast expanding tapestry the edges of which unfurl in
space and time far beyond what we are capable of seeing? Je est
un autre, the French visionary poet Arthur Rimbaud famously
wrote. I is someone else. Let's amend that statement to proclaim: je vous suis. I am you.

Me-in-you. You-in-me. We in each other. I pray to be able,
clearly and on a daily basis, to see and to act according to such
utter and ineradicable interconnectedness.

For Not Knowing

Almighty LORD, incline Thine ear to hear this day a confession: we sometimes do not feel real. That is, when we take the time to reflect upon our existence, we grow fearful, in part because we are unable to sum it up, to define what we are in terms that we find—due to the fractured nature of our lives—acceptable. For instance, LORD, we don't know where our selves are located, or if, individually, we could be said to "have" or "possess" a self, at least in the way that our ancestors thought of their selves as having "souls." We don't know what the word "soul" means, really, can't fathom it, can't really understand the word "spirit," either, can only imagine a gaseous dissolute form, a transparent ether-like substance that plays some magical part in animating our bodies, can't understand how a brain stores and maintains its memories or how it perceived sensations, or how awareness works, or where it goes when the body that has housed it dies. And indeed, we get more than a little weirded out that this primary mode of being cannot not be explained, because of course we've taken science and biology classes, both in religious and public institutions, and we've argued in our heads with our astronomy professor, who claimed to believe only in things he could see and claimed all humans were made of star stuff, and we then later reconciled this with the idea that You had maybe used this to form people and trees and animals and water and air and everything else and that this idea was just no less incredible or as a giant man in space reaching down for a handful of clay and shaping and then animating it with his magical breath, but neither of these explanations for how humans and other animals came into being shed any light whatsoever on what, exactly, consciousness is, much less life itself, since, when it comes right down to it, everything that happens to us happens to us on the inside, and is not, as it turns out, locatable or transferable or viewable to anyone else but the "we" who experience our own mental functions. There is, then, so much that we do not know, so much that we cannot know. And so we ask that we might learn not to fear this unknowingness. Remind us that not knowing, sometimes, is a good thing, and that You wouldn't be You if we could sum you up, if we could know the mystery of Thy ways. And maybe what we mean to say right now, oh LORD, is: forgive those of us who say you don't exist, just as you forgive those of us who do.

Our Thanks for Nothing

Dear LORD, we gather here this day to offer our thanks for nothing. If you recall, before the beginning there was nothing and it was good. The earth without form and void and darkness upon the face of the deep and this together was good, in fact, it was very good. Perhaps we did not appreciate the goodness of this time, perhaps we took it for granted. We apologize. It was wrong of us to take the goodness of this time for granted. We can see that now.

And then came the light and there was light and things were less good. Then calling the light Day and the darkness Night and a firmament in the midst of the waters and the division of waters from waters and things were still good, though not quite as good as before. Then the dry land appeared and you called it Earth and then grass, the herb yielding seed, and the fruit tree yielding fruit after his kind and this was fine. Then if we skip ahead a little bit the waters brought forth abundantly the moving creature that hath life, and fowl that may fly above the earth in the open firmament of heaven and even this was acceptable for a time and a good time it was. Where we get into some trouble, what might be called the beginning of the end, is when you BLESSED them and said Be fruitful and multiply and fill the waters and then the earth brought forth the living creature, cattle and such, and everything that creepeth upon the earth after his kind. Had we left well enough alone at this point then things might still be good, but alas, in your infinite wisdom you made man in your image, after your likeness and they had dominion over the fish of the sea, the fowl of the air, and over the cattle, over all the earth and over every creeping thing that creepeth upon the earth and things got a lot less good. Still, though, even still, it was paradise and the air was fresh and good to breathe and the water was clean and good to drink, and still there was a great deal of nothing to give thanks for, but where things went past the point of rescue was after the blessing and the going forth to be fruitful and multiply and replenishing the earth and subduing it and having dominion over everything and now where the hell are we. Six billion strong and there is everything and nothing every day, relentlessly, nothing today, nothing tomorrow, nothing the day after that along with everything else. But this nothing today, tomorrow, and the day after could never be confused for that long ago absolute nothing, like it was before the beginning, our time of sweet oblivion. For years there was nothing and it was good and we neglected to give thanks for this nothing and have been paying for it ever since. Allow us to apologize once more. We are contrite. We are regretful. We are human. And we humbly beseech thee to please return us to our long lost nothingness at your earliest convenience. We thank you in advance.

Prayer (I)

Every day I want to speak with you. And every day something more important
calls for my attention—the drugstore, the beauty products, the luggage

I need to buy for the trip.
Even now I can hardly sit here

among the falling piles of paper and clothing, the garbage trucks outside
already screeching and banging.

The mystics say you are as close as my own breath.
Why do I flee from you?

My days and nights pour through me like complaints
and become a story I forgot to tell.

Help me. Even as I write these words I am planning
to rise from the chair as soon as I finish this sentence.

Prayer (II)

Let the books on our shelves rest in an ordered chaos.
Let the chaos leave spaces of light.
Let us hold our hands up to the light.
Let the light reflect off our fingernails,
its glow reminding us of the beginning of time.
Let us begin a thousand times
an hour; keep us nimble, awake
a quiet fire.

•

Something moves inside me, stops, leaps
when he slams
the car door shut in the cold and walks
towards my white window.
I forget the argument, his hand is turning
the door handle, the ringing of his keys.

•

I am like the girl-becoming-woman in the long white dress in the movie,
after rocking and breathing, flushed,
into her prayer-book, into her mother's hair,
she is now frightened,
enclosed in a room with the man she loves
for the first time;
he hangs his hat on a hook,
she stands in the corner, her eyes darting, searching, not knowing, searching
for a problem.

•

Let the wildness be warm and circling like the foxes in the night streets.
Let the night shine on the hill. Let us be
without doubt, without certainty,
loving best what we can't see. Let us wonder,
asking.

Prayer (for an End)

When the time comes
my back will not be turned.

I'll throw down my gun,
refuse to march ten paces.

I want to watch the bullet come,
skidding silver into skin.

Next life I'll be
a well-cared for dog,

a blade of grass
on a mountaintop in Sweden,

my unborn daughter's son,
a real poet.

The end is my beginning
like reading Hebrew,

the last page,
my first.

I shoot to the end
so that I know how to live,

so that I know
how words will leave me.

Alphabetical List of Titles and Authors

Cruise with Her Parents" George Bishop, Jr.

"For Beds" Matthew Vollmer

"For Children at Bedtime" John Haskell

"For Everyday Punks" Robert Kenagy

"For Faithless Wives, on the Nightly Removal of Prosthetic Limbs" Christian TeBordo

"For Flight Attendants Giving Safety Speeches" Matthew Vollmer

"For Glampers" Benjamin Samuel

"For Gluten" Wendy Brenner

"For Guns" Matthew Vollmer

"For Heated Swimming Pools" Amy Fusselman

"For Hypochondriacs" Christy Crutchfield

"For Lost Phones" Lee Klein

"For Lubbock" Charles McLeod

"For Men Named Nancy" Catherine Lacey

"For Mild Paranoia" Christy Crutchfield

"For Mothers Who Dread the Dentist" Lauren Jensen

"For My Daughter, Who Does Not Exist" Dan Albergotti

"For Not Knowing" Matthew Vollmer

"For People Who Are Seeing their New Rental for the First Time" Nic Brown

"For Post-Interview Job Candidates" Nic Brown

"For Saturday Mail" Gabe Durham

"For the Battering of Heart in the Matter of Our Daughter, That She May Rise and Stand, O'erthrown by Thee and Made New" Joseph Salvatore

"For the Department Store Santa" Sean Conaway

"For the Driver of the Oversized Load Escort Vehicle" Courtney Maum

"For the Drivers of Tractor Trailers" Matthew Vollmer

"For the Good and Proper Use of Money" Matthew Vollmer

"For the Harmless Yet Disgusting Parasitic Nematodes That Last Week Briefly Infected Our Children" Jensen Beach

"For the Hostess on the Eve of an Ill-Conceived Party" Brenda Miller

"For the Middle School Boy and His Intemperate Prurience" Nate Liederbach

"For the Moth, But Also for the Spider" Caitlin Horrocks

"For the Mysterious Source of Life" Clyde Edgerton

"For the Newly Minted Ph.D. in English Literature"
Jaime Clarke

"For the Non-Participant Audience Members on *The Price Is Right*" Nathan Blake

"For the Preteen Girl" Mieke Eerkens

"For the Reunion of the White Stripes" William Giraldi

"For the Running Man" Matthew Vollmer

"For the Shy, Sad Children of Divorce, Who Never Wanted to Go Fishing in the First Place" Ian Stansel

"For the Spudnuts, As They Take to the Sky"
Matthew Gavin Frank

"For the Translator" Michelle Kyoto Crowson

"For the Unlikely Heroes of Apocalypse Movies"
Leslie Jamison

"For the Unseeable Child in the Rear-Facing Safety Seat"
Weston Cutter

"For the Woman of a Certain Age Joining Match.com [again]"
Brenda Miller

"For the Woman Who Bought a Groupon..."
A. K. Benninghofen

"For Those Currently Much Drunker Than They Meant to Get" Catherine Lacey

"For Those Haunted by Deceased Parents, Lost Youth, Missed Connections, Misspent Friendships, Spent Looks, Dropped Balls, Roads Not Taken, Words Not Spoken, Words Spoken, Dampened Passions, Failures of Both Business and Imagination, Bad Calls, Mixed Bags, Sagging Flesh, Spilt Milk, Bad Blood, and Random Acts of Unkindness" Dawn Raffel

"For Those Hung-over on Tuesday" Dylan Nice

"For Those Loitering In Front of Quik Check, Madera, Pennsylvania, July 1998" Dylan Nice

"For Those Perusing Souvenirs Sold in Gas Stations or Truck Stops" Will Kaufman

"For Those Who Do Not Want to Get Angry at Their Very Nice Boyfriends" Catherine Lacey

"For Those Who Perpetrated the Moon Landing Hoax" Gabriel Blackwell

"For Very Thirsty Souls Who Are Out of Beer After the Liquor Stores Have Closed" Amber Sparks

"For Video Game Characters Who Are Running Out of Hit Points Right in the Middle of the Last Boss Fight" Amber Sparks

"For Vince McMahon and the Tending of the Flock" Brian Oliu

"Four Prayers for the New Year" Ravi Shankar

"New Year's Prayer" Jonterri Gadson

Acknowledgments

"An Exhortation: Against Dread" will appear in *The Normal School.*

"An Agnostic or Maybe Atheist Hindu's Plea for Sanity, Or If That's Not Possible, Some Snacks" by V. V. Ganeshananthan originally appeared in *Drunken Boat 20.*

"Circus Prayer," by Scott Loring Sanders, originally appeared in *Sweet.*

"Evening Prayer," by Alicia Jo Rabins, was originally commissioned by composer S. Beth May.

"For Actors in Pornographic Films," "For Beds," and "For Not Knowing" originally appeared at *New Orleans Review* (web). "For Beds" later appeared in *The Pushcart Prize Anthology 2015.*

"For Alien Abductees" by Robert Kenagy appeared in *Squalorly.*

"For Drivers of Tractor Trailers," "For Guns," and "For the Running Man" by Matthew Vollmer originally appeared in *The Pinch.*

"For Flight Attendants Giving Safety Speeches" by Matthew Vollmer originally appeared at *Airplane Reading.*

"For Gluten" by Wendy Brenner originally appeared in *The Sun Magazine.*

"For Lost Phones" by Lee Klein originally appeared at McSweeney's Internet Tendency.

"For Mild Paranoia" by Christy Crutchfield originally appeared in *Green Mountains Review*.

"For My Daughter, Who Does Not Exist" by Dan Albergotti, originally appeared as "Prayer for My Daughter, Who Does Not Exist" in *The Boatloads* (BOA editions, 2008)

"For Target" by Chad Davidson originally appeared as "Target" in *From The Last Predicta*. Carbondale, IL: Southern Illinois UP, 2008.

"For the Battering of Heart in the Matter of Our Daughter, That She May Rise and Stand, O'erthrown by Thee and Made New" by Joseph Salvatore, will appear in *Epiphany*.

"For the Moth, But Also for the Spider" by Caitlin Horrocks originally appeared in *Memorious*.

"For the Shy, Sad Children of Divorce, Who Never Wanted to Go Fishing in the First Place" by Ian Stansel originally appeared in *Revolver*.

"For the Woman Who Bought a Groupon..." by A. K. Benninghofen originally appeared in *Passages North*.

"For Very Thirsty Souls Who Are Out of Beer After the Liquor Stores Have Closed" and "For Video Game Characters Who Are Running Out of Hit Points Right in the Middle of the Last Boss Fight" by Amber Sparks originally appeared in *Moon City Review*.

"For Vince McMahon and the Tending of the Flock," by Brian Oliu, originally appeared in *storySouth*.

"Post-Game-Day Blessing" by Erika Meitner originally appeared in *The Kenyon Review*

"Prayer (for an End)" by Hadara Bar-Nadav appears in *A Glass of Milk to Kiss Goodnight*. Chesterfield: Margie/Intuit House, 2007 and was originally published in *Seattle Review* as "The Never-Ending End."

"What is Good: A Meditation" by Ricky Moody originally appeared as "A Short Primer on Philosophy" in *AGNI*.

"For the Unlikely Heroes of Apocalypse Movies" by Leslie Jamison appeared in partial and altered form in both the magazine *Bright Wall Dark Room* and in *Such Mean Estate* (with photos by Ryan Spencer, powerHouse Books, April 2015).

"A Prayer for Glamers" by Benjamin Samuel originally appeared in *Midnight Breakfast*.

Contributors' Notes

Dan Albergotti ("For My Daughter, Who Does Not Exist") is the author of *The Boatloads* (BOA Editions, 2008) and *Millennial Teeth* (Southern Illinois University Press, 2014), as well as a limited-edition chapbook, *The Use of the World* (Unicorn Press, 2013). His poems have appeared in *The Cincinnati Review, Five Points, The Southern Review, The Virginia Quarterly Review,* and *Pushcart Prize XXXIII,* as well as other journals and anthologies. A graduate of the MFA program at UNC Greensboro and former poetry editor of *The Greensboro Review,* Albergotti is a professor of English at Coastal Carolina University in Conway, South Carolina.

Kate Angus's ("Peace Prayer") work has appeared in *Indiana Review, Subtropics, Court Green, The Awl, The Millions, Verse Daily, Best New Poets 2010* and *Best New Poets 2014,* among other places. She is the recipient of A Room of Her Own Foundation's "Orlando" Prize, *The Southeast Review*'s Narrative Nonfiction prize and an artists residency on the Wildfjords trail in Iceland. A former Writer in Residence at Interlochen Arts Academy, she currently lives in New York where she is a founding editor of Augury Books and serves as the Creative Writing Advisor for The Mayapple Center for Arts and Humanities.

Hadara Bar-Nadav ("Prayer (for an End)") is the author of *Lullaby (with Exit Sign),* awarded the Saturnalia Books Poetry Prize (Saturnalia Books, 2013); *The Frame Called Ruin* (New Issues, 2012), Runner Up for the Green Rose Prize; and *A Glass of Milk to Kiss Goodnight (Margie/*Intuit House, 2007), awarded the Margie Book Prize. Her chapbook, *Show Me Yours (Laurel Review/*Green Tower Press, 2010), was awarded the Midwest Poets Series Award. She is also co-author of the textbook *Writing Poems, 8th ed.* (Pearson, 2011). Hadara is currently an Associate Professor of English at the University of Missouri-Kansas City.

Jensen Beach ("For the Harmless Yet Disgusting Parasitic Nematodes That Last Week Briefly Infected Our Children") is the author of two collections of short stories, *For Out of the Heart Proceed* (Dzanc Books) and the forthcoming *Swallowed by the Cold* (Graywolf Press). His stories and essays have recently appeared in *A Public Space, Cincinnati Review* and *Ninth Letter.* Currently, he teaches in the BFA program at Johnson State College. He's a webeditor at *Hobart* and the fiction editor of *Green Mountains Review.* He lives in Vermont with his wife and children.

A.K. Benninghofen ("For the Woman Who Bought a Groupon...") grew up in the Mississippi Delta. She spent the first part of her adult life living in New York City and Los Angeles pursuing a career as an actress, which is to say, she has a lot of restaurant experience. She now lives happily with her husband and two small children in Beer City, USA (otherwise known as Asheville, NC.) A.K.'s fiction has appeared or is forthcoming in *Evergreen Review, Monkeybicycle, Connotation Press, Necessary Fiction* and *Deep South.* In 2012, A.K. was awarded a Regional Artist Project Grant by the North Carolina Arts Council. Currently, she is at work on her first book, a collection of linked stories titled "Landmine Maps of the Hospitality State."

Gabriel Blackwell ("For Those Who Perpetrated the Moon Landing Hoax") is the author of three books, including, most recently, *The Natural Dissolution of Fleeting-Improvised-Men.* His essays and fictions have appeared in *Conjunctions, Tin House, DIAGRAM, Puerto del Sol, Portland Review,* and many others. With Matthew Olzmann, he is the editor of *The Collagist.*

George Bishop, Jr. ("For a Teenage Girl Embarking Upon a Weeklong Carnival Cruise with Her Parents" and "For Aging Rock Stars") holds a BA from Loyola University in New Orleans, an MFA from the University of North Carolina in Wilmington, and an MA from the School for International Training in Vermont. He has lived and taught in Slovakia, Turkey, Indonesia, Azerbaijan, Kyrgyzstan, India, and Japan. His first novel, *Letter to My Daughter* was published by Ballantine Books in 2010; his second, *The Night of the Comet*, also with Ballantine, was named one of the best books of 2013 by Kirkus Reviews. In a past life he starred as Murphy Gilcrease, the teenage vampire, in the 1988 New World Pictures release *Teen Vamp*.

Nathan Blake's ("For the Non-Participant Audience Members on *The Price Is Right*") chapbook *Going Home Nowhere and Fast* is available from Winged City Press. He is currently an MFA candidate at Virginia Tech.

Wendy Brenner ("For Gluten" and "For a Friend Who Has Deactivated Her Facebook Account") is the author of two books of short fiction, *Large Animals in Everyday Life*, which won the Flannery O'Connor Award, and *Phone Calls From the Dead*. Her short stories and essays have appeared in *Best American Essays, Allure, Travel & Leisure, Seventeen, Best American Magazine Writing, New Stories From the South*, and many other magazines, journals, and anthologies. She teaches writing at University of North Carolina Wilmington and serves as a Contributing Editor for *The Oxford American*. She is currently completing a collection of essays.

Nic Brown ("For Post-Interview Job Candidates" and "For People Who Are Seeing their New Rental for the First Time") is the author of the novels *In Every Way, Doubles*, and *Floodmarkers*, which was selected as an Editor's Choice by *The New York Times Book Review*. His writing has appeared in *The New York Times, the Harvard Review, Glimmer Train*, and *Epoch*, among many other publications. A graduate of the Iowa Writers' Workshop and Columbia University, he has been the John and Renee Grisham Writer in Residence at the University of Mississippi and is currently an assistant professor of English at Clemson University.

Scott Cheshire ("An Exortation: Against Dread") earned his MFA from Hunter College. His work has been published in *AGNI*, *Electric Literature*, *Harper's*, *Slice*, and the Picador anthology *The Book of Men*. His first novel *High as the Horses' Bridles* is published by Henry Holt.

Jaime Clarke ("For the Newly Minted Ph.D. in English Literature") is a graduate of the University of Arizona and holds an MFA from Bennington College. He is the author of the novels *We're So Famous*, *Vernon Downs*, *and World Gone Water*, editor of the anthologies *Don't You Forget About Me: Contemporary Writers on the Films of John Hughes*, *Conversations with Jonathan Lethem*, and *Talk Show: On the Couch with Contemporary Writers*; and co-editor of the anthologies *No Near Exit: Writers Select Their Favorite Work from Post Road Magazine* (with Mary Cotton), and *Boston Noir 2: The Classics* (with Dennis Lehane and Mary Cotton). He is a founding editor of the literary magazine *Post Road*, now published at Boston College, and co-owner, with his wife, of *Newtonville Books*, an independent bookstore in Boston.

Sean Conaway ("For the Department Store Santa") doesn't believe in God, at least not the popular notion of him, but he does believe in prayer, particularly on a sub-atomic level. Those neurons firing between prayerful synapses are mirrored somewhere, nearby or in the spooky distance. They linger. They gather and swirl.

Stanley Crawford ("A Sophist's Prayer") divides his time between writing and farming in Northern New Mexico, where he and his wife RoseMary have lived since 1969. He's the author of seven novels, among which is *The Canyon* (University of New Mexico Press), *Seed* (FC2/University of Alabama Press),

The Log of the S.S. The Mrs Unguentine (Dalkey Archive Press, Champaign and London), and three works of nonfiction about Northern New Mexico, including *A Garlic Testament: Seasons on a Small New Mexico Farm* (The University of New Mexico Press, Albuquerque). *Intimacy*, a novella, will be published in 2016 by FC2/University of Alabama Press. Crawford has been the recipient of two NEA Writing Fellowships and a three-year Lila Wallace-Reader's Digest Writer's Award, and has held residencies at the MacDowell Colony, the Bellagio Study Center, and Centrum in Port Townsend, Washington. He has taught at the Institute of American Indian Arts in Santa Fe, the U-Mass/Amherst, and Colorado College in Colorado Springs.

Michelle Kyoko Crowson ("For the Translator") is a PhD student in Comparative Literature at the University of Oregon. Her work has appeared most recently in *Foothill, Oregon Quarterly, Silk Road,* and *Permafrost.*

Christy Crutchfield ("For Hypochondriacs" and "For Mild Paranoia") is the author of the novel *How to Catch a Coyote* (Publishing Genius Press). Her writing has appeared in *Mississippi Review online, Salt Hill Journal, the Collagist,* and others. Originally form Atlanta, she writes and teaches in Western Massachusetts.

Weston Cutter ("For the Unseeable Child in the Rear-Facing Safety Seat") is from Minnesota and is the author of *You'd Be a Stranger, Too* and the poetry chapbooks *All Black Everything* and *Enough.*

Chad Davidson ("For Target") is the author of *From the Fire Hills* (2014), *The Last Predicta* (2008), and *Consolation Miracle* (2003), all three from Southern Illinois UP, as well as co-author with Gregory Fraser of two textbooks, including *Writing Poetry: Creative* and *Critical Approaches* (Palgrave Macmillan, 2009). His poems have appeared in *AGNI*, *Boston Review*, *DoubleTake*, *The Paris Review*, *Ploughshares*, *Virginia Quarterly Review*, and many others. He is a professor of literature and creative writing at the University of West Georgia near Atlanta.

Gabe Durham ("For Saturday Mail") is the author of the novel *Fun Camp* and the Editor of *Book Fight Books*, a series of books about video games. He and his projects have been featured in *The Onion A.V. Club*, *Nylon Guys Magazine*, *The Brooklyn Rail*, *Kotaku*, *Largehearted Boy*, and Julie Klausner's "How Was Your Week" podcast. He lives in Los Angeles.

Mieke Eerkens ("For the Preteen Girl") is a Dutch-American writer who grew up divided between the foothills of California and the canals of the Netherlands. She is a graduate of the University of Iowa's MFA program in Nonfiction Writing and her work has appeared in publications such as *The Atlantic*, *Guernica*, *The Los Angeles Review of Books*, *The Rumpus*, *Creative Nonfiction*, and the Norton anthology *Fakes: An Anthology of Pseudo-Interviews, Faux-Lectures, Quasi-Letters, "Found" Texts, and Other Fraudulent Artifacts*, among others.

Clyde Edgerton ("For the Mysterious Source of Life") is the author of ten novels and two books of nonfiction. He is the Thomas S. Kenan III Distinguished Professir of Creative Writing at UNC Wilmington and a member of the Fellowship of Southern Writers. His latest book is *Papadaddy's Book for New Fathers*.

Matthew Gavin Frank ("For the Spudnuts, As They Take to the Sky") is the author of the nonfiction books, *Preparing the Ghost: An Essay Concerning the Giant Squid and Its First Photographer*, *Pot Farm*, and *Barolo*, the poetry books, *The Morrow Plots*, *Warranty in Zulu*, and *Sagittarius Agitprop*, and the chapbooks, *Four Hours to Mpumalanga* and *Aardvark*. His essay collection/cookbook,

The Mad Feast, is forthcoming in 2016 from W.W. Norton: Liveright. He teaches at Northern Michigan University, where he is the Nonfiction Editor of *Passages North*. This winter, he tempered his gin with two droplets (per 750ml) of tincture of odiferous whitefish liver. For health.

Amy Fusselman ("For Heated Swimming Pools") is the author of *The Pharmacist's Mate, 8*, and *Savage Park*. She is the publisher at *Ohio Edit*.

Jonterri Gadson ("New Year's Prayer") is the author of the chapbook, *Pepper Girl* (YesYes Books, 2012). She is the recipient of fellowships/scholarships from Bread Loaf, Cave Canem, and the University of Virginia's Creative Writing MFA program. Her poetry is forthcoming or published in *Los Angeles Review, The Collagist, PANK*, and other journals. She currently serves as the Herbert W. Martin Post-Graduate Creative Writing Fellow at University of Dayton in Ohio.

V.V. Ganeshananthan ("An Agnostic or Maybe Atheist Hindu's Plea for Sanity, Or If That's Not Possible, Some Snacks") is a fiction writer and journalist. Her debut novel, *Love Marriage,* is set in Sri Lanka and its diasporas, was longlisted for the Orange Prize, and was named one of *Washington Post* Book World's Best of 2008. She is a 2014 National Endowment for the Arts Literature Fellow, and a 2014-2015 Fellow at the Radcliffe Institute for Advanced Study at Harvard. She previously taught at the University of Michigan, and in 2015 will begin teaching at the University of Minnesota. She believes in things sometimes, and is currently at work on the problem of evil and a second novel, an excerpt of which appears in *Best American Nonrequired Reading 2014.*

William Giraldi ("For the Reunion of the White Stripes") is author of the novels *Busy Monsters* (Norton, 2011) and *Hold the*

Dark (Norton, 2014). He is fiction editor for the journal *AGNI* at Boston University.

Ani Gjika ("The Lord's Prayer") moved from Albania to the U.S. at age 18 and studied poetry writing at Simmons College and Boston University. She is the recipient of a 2010 Robert Pinsky Global Fellowship and winner of a 2010 Robert Fitzgerald Translation Prize. Her first book, *Bread on Running Waters*, (Fenway Press, 2013), was a finalist for the 2011 Anthony Hecht Poetry Prize and 2011 May Sarton New Hampshire Book Prize. Her poems and translations have appeared or are forthcoming in *AGNI Online, Ploughshares, Seneca Review, Salamander, Silk Road Review, From the Fishouse* and elsewhere.

Eve Grubin ("Prayer (II)") is the author of a book of poems, *Morning Prayer*, which appeared in 2006 from the Sheep Meadow Press. Her poems have appeared or are forthcoming in many literary journals and magazines, including *The American Poetry Review, PN Review, The Virginia Quarterly Review, The New Republic*, and *Conjunctions*, where her chapbook-size group of poems was featured and introduced by Fanny Howe. Her essays have appeared in various magazines and anthologies including, *The Veil: Women Writers on Its History, Lore, and Politics* (U of CA Press, 2009) and *This-World Company: Essays on Jean Valentine* (U of Mich Press 2012). Eve was the programs director at the Poetry Society of America for five years. She has taught poetry at The New School University and in the graduate creative writing program at the City College of New York. She now teaches at New York University in London and is a tutor at the Poetry School. She is the poet in residence at at the London School of Jewish Studies.

John Haskell ("For Children at Bedtime") is the author of a short-story collection, *I Am Not Jackson Pollock* (FSG, 2003) and the novels, *American Purgatorio* (FSG, 2005) and *Out of My Skin*

(FSG, 2009). His stories and essays have appeared on the radio (The Next Big Thing, Studio 360), in books (*The Show You'll Never Forget, Heavy Rotation*), and in magazines (including *A Public Space, n+1, Conjunctions*, and *McSweeney's*). He is a recipient of a 2009 Guggenheim fellowship, was recently awarded a NYFA grant. He has taught at Columbia University, Cal Arts, and the University of Leipzig.

Bob Hicok's ("Prayer of the Agnostic") latest book is *Elegy Owed* (Copper Canyon, 2013).

Caitlin Horrocks ("For the Moth, But Also for the Spider") is author of the story collection *This Is Not Your City*. Her work appears in *The New Yorker, Best American Short Stories, PEN/O. Henry Prize Stories, Pushcart Prize* and elsewhere. She is fiction editor of *The Kenyon Review* and teaches at Grand Valley State University in Grand Rapids, Michigan.

Marie Howe ("Prayer (I)") is the author of three volumes of poetry, *The Kingdom of Ordinary Time* (2008); *The Good Thief* (1998); and *What the Living Do* (1997), and is the co-editor of a book of essays, *In the Company of My Solitude: American Writing from the AIDS Pandemic* (1994). Stanley Kunitz selected Howe for a Lavan Younger Poets Prize from the American Academy of Poets. She has, in addition, been a fellow at the Bunting Institute at Radcliffe College and a recipient of NEA and Guggenheim fellowships. Her poems have appeared in *The New Yorker, The Atlantic, Poetry, Agni, Ploughshares, Harvard Review,* and *The Partisan Review,* among others. Currently, Howe teaches creative writing at Sarah Lawrence College, Columbia, and New York University. She is the 2012-2014 Poet Laureate of New York State.

Leslie Jamison ("For the Unlikely Heroes of Apocalypse Movies") is the author of a novel, *The Gin Closet*, and a collection of essays, *The Empathy Exams*. Her mother, Joanne Leslie, is the archdeacon of the Episcopal Diocese of Los Angeles.

Lauren Jensen ("A Bidding Prayer for Those Who Pray," "By the Power of All that Is Seen and Unseen" and "For Mothers Who Dread the Dentist") lives in Eugene, Oregon.

Will Kaufman's ("For Those Perusing Souvenirs Sold in Gas Stations or Truck Stops") work has appeared in *The Collagist, Unstuck, PANK, Lightspeed*, and a number of other journals. Links to his published work can be found at www.kaufman-writes.com. He has an MFA in Creative Writing from the University of Utah, an MA from UC Davis, and attended the Clarion Science Fiction and Fantasy Writer's Workshop in 2013.

Rob Kenagy's ("For Alien Abductees" and "For Everday Punks") work has appeared in *Best of the Net 2013, Vinyl, Hobart (web), Squalorly, Forklift, Ohio*, and elsewhere. He writes and records music as Ganges.

Lee Klein ("For Lost Phones") is the author of *The Shimmering Go-Between: A Novel* and *Thanks and Sorry and Good Luck: Rejection Letters from the Eyeshot Outbox*, a collection of unconventional declines he sent in response to submissions between 2002 and 2012 while editing Eyeshot.net. He lives in South Philadelphia.

Catherine Lacey ("For Men Named Nancy," "For Those Currently Much Drunker Than They Meant to Get," and "For Those Who Do Not Want to Get Angry at Their Very Nice Boyfriends") is the author of *Nobody Is Ever Missing* and two more books of fiction forthcoming from FSG in the somewhat near future.

J. Robert Lennon ("Prayer: Friday Night at Hot Slice") is the author of two story collections, *See You in Paradise* and *Pieces For The Left Hand*, and seven novels, including *Mailman*, *Familiar*, and *Happyland*. He teaches writing at Cornell University.

Ariel Lewiton ("For the Tin Man") lives in New York. Her essays and stories have appeared in *The Los Angeles Review of Books*, *Vice.com*, *The Paris Review* Daily, *Tin House* online, *Ninth Letter*, and elsewhere.

Nate Liederbach ("For the Middle School Boy and His Intemperate Prurience") is the author of the prose collections *Doing a Bit of Bleeding* (Ghost Road), Negative Spaces (Elik), *Beasts You'll Never See* (Noemi, forthcoming), and *Tongues of Men and of Angels: Nonfictions Ataxia* (sunnyoutside, forthcoming). He lives in Eugene, Oregon, and Olympia, Washington.

Samuel Ligon ("For My Neighbor's Quick, Painless Death") is the author of a book of stories, *Drift and Swerve*, and a novel, *Safe in Heaven Dead*. His stories have appeared in *New England Review*, *Prairie Schooner*, *Alaska Quarterly Review*, *Post Road*, *The Quarterly*, and elsewhere. He teaches at Eastern Washington University in Spokane, and is the editor of *Willow Springs*.

Robert Lopez ("Our Thanks for Nothing") is the author of two novels, *Part of the World* and *Kamby Bolongo Mean River*, and a collection of short fiction, *Asunder*. *Good People*, a collection, is forthcoming from Bellevue Literary Press in 2016 and *All Back Full*, a novel, is forthcoming from Dzanc in 2016, as well. He lives in Brooklyn.

Courtney Maum ("For the Driver of the Oversized Load Escort Vehicle") is the author of the novel *I Am Having So Much Fun Here Without You* from Simon & Schuster, and the chapbook, *Notes from Mexico* from The Cupboard Press. She's also the humor columnist behind the "Celebrity Book Review" on *Electric*

Literature and a satirical advice giver for *Tin House*. She lives in the Berkshires of Massachusetts.

Aaron McCollough ("A Prayer Cycle to Be Uttered by Five Enemies") is the Editorial Director of Michigan Publishing (which includes the University of Michigan Press). His books include *Underlight* (Ugly Duckling Presse, 2012); *No Grave Can Hold My Body Down* (Ahsahta Press, 2011); *Little Ease* (Ahsahta Press, 2006); *Double Venus* (Salt Publishing, 2003); and *Welkin* (Ahsahta Press, 2002).

Charles McLeod ("For Lubbock") is the author of a novel, *American Weather*, and two collections of stories: *National Treasures*, and the forthcoming *Settlers of Unassigned Lands*. He's the recipient of a Pushcart Prize and fellowships from the University of Virginia, the Fine Arts Work Center in Provincetown, and San Jose State University, where he was a Steinbeck Fellow. His website is www.charles-mcleod.com.

Erika Meitner ("Post-Game-Day Blessing") is the author, most recently, of *Copia* (BOA Editions, 2014), and *Ideal Cities* (HarperCollins, 2010), which was a 2009 National Poetry Series winner. Her poems have been published in *Best American Poetry 2011, Ploughshares, The New Republic, Virginia Quarterly Review, APR, Tin House*, and elsewhere. She is currently an associate professor of English at Virginia Tech, where she teaches in the MFA program.

Brenda Miller ("For the Woman of a Certain Age Joining Match.com [again]" and "For the Hostess on the Eve of an Ill-Conceived Party") is the author of three essay collections: *Listening Against the Stone* (Skinner House Books, 2012), *Blessing of the Animals* (Eastern Washington University Press, 2009), and *Season of the Body* (Sarabande Books, 2002). She has also co-authored *Tell It Slant: Creating, Refining and Publishing Cre-*

ative Nonfiction (McGraw Hill, 2012) and *The Pen and The Bell: Mindful Writing in a Busy World* (Skinner House Books, 2012). Her work has received six Pushcart Prizes. She is a Professor of English at Western Washington University and serves as Editor-in-Chief of the *Bellingham Review*. Her website is www.brendamillerwriter.com.

Rick Moody ("What Is Good: A Meditation") is the author of five novels, three collections of stories, a memoir, and a collection of essays on music. He also sings and plays in The Wingdale Community Singers.

Liz Moore ("The Prayers of the Person") is the author of the novels *The Words of Every Song* (Broadway Books, 2007) and *Heft* (W.W. Norton, 2012). She is also a professor of writing at Holy Family University in Philadelphia, where she lives. Her third novel is forthcoming from W.W. Norton.

Dylan Nice ("For Those Hung-over on Tuesday" and "For Those Loitering In Front of Quik Check, Madera, Pennsylvania, July 1998") is author of the short story collection, *Other Kinds*. His fiction and essays have appeared in *NOON, MAKE, Hobart, The Indiana Review,* and elsewhere. He lives in Iowa Ciy, Iowa.

Brian Oliu ("For Vince McMahon and the Tending of the Flock") is originally from New Jersey & currently lives in Tuscaloosa, Alabama. He is the author of "So You Know It's Me," a series of Tuscaloosa Missed Connections, *Level End,* a collection of lyric essays about video game boss battles, & "Leave Luck to Heaven," an ode to 8-bit Nintendo games. He is working on a series of essays about professional wrestlers.

Alicia Jo Rabins' ("Evening Prayer") poems and nonfiction have appeared in *AmericanPoetry Review, Ploughshares, Boston Review,*

6x6, *Court Green, Kveller, Huffington Post*, and anthologies from NYU Press and Knopf. She is the winner of the 2015 American Poetry Review/Honickman First Book Prize for her debut collection, *Divinity School*, to be published by Copper Canyon Press. Alicia holds an MFA in Poetry from Warren Wilson and a MA in Jewish Women's Studies from the Jewish Theological Seminary. In addition to Alicia's work as a writer she is a composer, performer and Torah teacher, and tours internationally with her band, Girls in Trouble, a song cycle about the complicated lives of Biblical women. She is based in Portland, Oregon. Her website is www.aliciajo.com.

Dawn Raffel's ("For Those of Haunted by Deceased Parents... etc") most recent book is *The Secret Life of Objects*. She is also the author of two story collections and a novel. She is up to the eyeballs in research for her next book, which is narrative nonfiction.

Wendy Rawlings ("To God Almighty That I Have Never Believed In, Especially Since This Entity Saw Fit to Take My Best Friend Rosemarie Who Had Just Finished Med School at Johns Hopkins When She Was Killed in a Horrible Car Accident") is an atheist and the author of two books, *The Agnostics* and *Come Back Irish*. Her work has appeared in *AGNI, Tin House, The Southern Review, The Cincinnati Review* and other magazines. She teaches in the MFA program at the University of Alabama.

Ryan Ridge ("Three Prayers for Artists") is the author of the story collection *Hunters & Gamblers*, the poetry collection *Ox*, as well as the chapbooks *Hey, it's America* and *22nd Century Man*. His latest book, *American Homes*, was released by the University of Michigan Press as part of their 21st Century Prose series. Recent work has appeared in *Tin House, McSweeney's Small Chair, FLAUNT Magazine, The Santa Monica Review, Sleepingfish, Hobart*, and elsewhere. A former editor-in-chief of *Faultline*, he now serves as managing editor for *Juked*.

Joseph Salvatore ("For the Battering of Heart in the Matter of Our Daughter, That She May Rise and Stand, O'erthrown by Thee and Made New") Joseph Salvatore is the author of the story collection *To Assume A Pleasing Shape* (BOA Editions, 2011) and the co-author of the college textbook *Understanding English Grammar* (Pearson, 2015). He is the book review editor for fiction and poetry at *The Brooklyn Rail* and a frequent contributor to *The New York Times Book Review*. His writing has appeared in *The Collagist, Dossier Journal, Epiphany, H.O.W. Journal, New York Tyrant, Open City, Post Road, Rain Taxi, Salt Hill, Sleeping Fish*, and *Willow Springs*, among others. He is an assistant professor of writing and literature at The New School, in New York City, where he founded the literary journal *LIT*. He lives in Queens. Visit him at www.josephsalvatore.com.

Benjamin Samuel ("For Glampers") is Electric Literature's editor-at-large and co-founder of its magazine Recommended Reading. His writing has appeared in *McSweeney's Internet Tendency, Flavorwire, Midnight Breakfast, The Huffington Post, The New York Daily News*, and the anthology *Paper Dreams: Writers and Editors on the American Literary Magazine*. He has an MFA from Brooklyn College and is still learning how to sleep in a tent.

Scott Loring Sanders ("Circus Prayer") has published two novels (*The Hanging Woods* and *Gray Baby*) with Houghton Mifflin, was the Writer-in-Residence at the Camargo Foundation in Cassis, France, and was twice a fellow at the Virginia Center for the Creative Arts. His short stories and essays have appeared in *Best American Mystery Stories 2014, Creative Nonfiction, Ellery Queen's Mystery Magazine*, and elsewhere. He teaches at Virginia Tech.

Ravi Shankar ("Four Prayers for the New Year") is the founding editor of Drunken Boat [http://www.drunkenboat.com] and the author/editor/publisher of 10 books and chapbooks of poetry, including W.W. Norton & Co.'s *Language for a New Century: Contemporary Poetry from Asia, the Middle East & Beyond* and *What Else Could it Be* (Carolina Wren, 2015). He has won a Pushcart Prize, appeared in *The New York Times, The Paris Review, The San Francisco Chronicle* and on BBC & NPR. He is a Professor of English at CCSU and teaches in the first international MFA Program at City University of Hong Kong.

Susan B.A. Somers-Willett ("For Signs") is the author of two award-winning books of poetry, *Quiver* (University of Georgia Press, 2009) and *Roam* (Crab Orchard Award Series, 2006), as well as a book of criticism, *The Cultural Politics of Slam Poetry* (University of Michigan Press, 2009). Her writing and criticism has been featured by several journals including *The Iowa Review, Virginia Quarterly Review, Gulf Coast, Poets & Writers, The New York Times,* and *The New Yorker*. Her collaborative multimedia documentary poetry series "Women of Troy" aired on PRI and BBC radio affiliates and received a Gracie Award from the Alliance for Women in Media. Her other honors include an NEA Creative Writing Fellowship, the Writers' League of Texas Book Award, and a Pushcart Prize. Visit her website at www.susansw.com.

Amber Sparks ("For Very Thirsty Souls Who Are Out of Beer After the Liquor Stores Have Closed" and "For Video Game Characters Who Are Running Out of Hit Points Right in the Middle of the Last Boss Fight") is the author of the short story collection *May We Shed These Human Bodies*, and the co-author, along with Robert Kloss and Matt Kish, of the hybrid text *The Desert Places*. Her second short story collection, *The Unfinished World and Other Stories*, will be published by Liveright in 2016. You can follow her ramblings @ambernoelle on Twitter.

Sasha Steensen ("Poems for Lent") is the author of three books of poetry: *House of Deer*, *A Magic Book*, *The Method*, all from Fence Books, as well as several chapbooks. She teaches Creative Writing at Colorado State University, where she also serves as a poetry editor for Colorado Review.

Sarah Strickley ("A Thanksgiving for the First Full Night of Sleep after the Birth of the First Child") is the recipient of a National Endowment for the Arts Creative Writing fellowship, an Ohio Arts grant, a Glenn Schaeffer Award from the International Institute of Modern Letters, and other honors. Her fiction and essays have appeared in *Oxford American* magazine, *A Public Space*, *the Harvard Review*, *Gulf Coast*, *The Southeast Review*, and elsewhere. She is a graduate of the Iowa Writers' Workshop and is currently a doctoral candidate in the University of Cincinnati's Department of English and Comparative Literature. She lives in Cincinnati with her husband, the writer Ian Stansel, and their daughter, Simone Esme.

Ian Stansel ("For the Shy, Sad Children of Divorce Who Never Wanted to Go Fishing in the First Place") is the author of a collection of short stories, *Everybody's Irish* (Five Chapters Books 2013), and his work has appeared in *Ploughshares*, *Salon*, *Ecotone*, *Cincinnati Review*, and elsewhere. He holds and MFA from the Iowa Writers' Workshop and a PhD from the University of Houston.

Christian TeBordo ("For Faithless Wives, on the Nightly Removal of Prosthetic Limbs") has published four books, most recently a collection of short fiction called *The Awful Possibilities*. His next one, *Toughlahoma*, was chosen for Rescue Press's Open Prose Series and will be available in spring 2015. He lives in Chicago where he is Director of the MFA Program and Assistant Professor of English at Roosevelt University.

Robert Uren ("A Creed," "The Blessing of a Civil Marriage," "The Celebration and Blessing of a Marriage") received an MFA in fiction from Virginia Tech. His stories have appeared in *Quarterly West* and *Post Road*. He and his son post internet videos as Couch Buddies Pictures.

Matthew Vollmer ("A Petition for Protection," "For Actors in Pornographic Films," "For Beds," "For the Drivers of Tractor Trailers," "For Flight Attendants Giving Safety Speeches," "For the Good and Proper Use of Money," "For Guns," "For Not Knowing," and "For the Running Man") is the author of two story collections—*Future Missionaries of America* and the forthcoming *Gateway to Paradise*—as well as a collection of essays—*inscriptions for headstones*. He is co-editor of *Fakes: An Anthology of Pseudo-Interviews, Faux-Lectures, Quasi-Letters, "Found" Texts, and Other Fraudulent Artifacts*. An editor for the University of Michigan Press' 21st Century Prose series, he is also an Assistant Professor at Virginia Tech, where he directs the undergraduate creative writing program.

CPSIA information can be obtained at www.ICGtesting.com
Printed in the USA
BVOW08s2341041215

429416BV00004B/92/P

9 781937 402761